Opening the Eye of New Awareness

Opening the Eye of New Awareness

Tenzin Gyatso,
the Fourteenth Dalai Lama

Translated by Donald S. Lopez Jr.,
with Jeffrey Hopkins

Wisdom Publications

First published in 1985
Second printing 1990

Wisdom Publications
361 Newbury Street, Boston, MA 02115, USA

British Library Cataloguing in Publication Data
Bstan-'dzin-rgya-mtsho. Dalai Lama XIV.
Opening the eye of new awareness.—(A Wisdom Intermediate Book. White Series)
1. Dge-lugs-pa (Sect)—Doctrines
I. Title II. Lopez, Donald S. III. Hopkins, Jeffrey IV. Legs bshad blo gsar mid'byed. English 294.3'923 BQ7630.

ISBN 0 86171 036 3

Set in Bembo 11 on 13 point
by Characters of Chard, Somerset
and printed and bound
in Singapore by Eurasia Press
(Offset) Pte. Ltd.

Contents

Translators' Preface

Opening the Eye of New Awareness (blo gsar mig 'byed), written by His Holiness the Dalai Lama in 1963, is intended to provide an overview of Buddhist theory and practice for those readers, both in the Tibetan community and in the West, who lack the time or opportunity to study the traditional Indian and Tibetan texts. Composed in a straightforward and compact style, the work introduces the major doctrines of Indian Buddhism as it was studied and practiced in Tibet. The Dalai Lama's citation of sources and his systematic presentation clearly establish the close connection between Tibetan Buddhism and late Indian Mahāyāna Buddhism, a historical connection that he describes in the final chapter. Hence, as the Dalai Lama points out, Tibetan Buddhism is not a "Lamaism" distinct from the main currents of Indian Buddhist thought.

Since writing *Opening the Eye of New Awareness,* the Dalai Lama has visited North America, Europe, South East Asia, Australia, Russia, Mongolia, and Japan, giving lectures and participating in cultural exchanges. These visits have been characterized by an ecumenical spirit, with the Dalai Lama emphasizing the importance of kindness and compassion for society. He has also spoken about Buddhist contributions to human culture.

Two lectures delivered in the U.S. have been included here, the first addressed to the Theosophical Society at Wheaton, Illinois in August, 1981, and the second to an assembly of meditators at the Zen Center in Green Gulch, California in October, 1979. Since the first demonstrates the Dalai Lama's altruistic social outlook and the second provides an overview of Tibetan structures of practice, these two talks provide a useful introduction to the translation of *Opening the Eye of New Awareness*.

The first lecture was translated and edited by Jeffrey Hopkins, and the second, spoken in English, was edited by Elizabeth Napper. *Opening the Eye of New Awareness* was translated by Donald S. Lopez, Jr. with Jeffrey Hopkins. The present translation is the second rendering of the Dalai Lama's text, the first having been published as *The Opening of the Wisdom Eye* (Wheaton, Illinois: Theosophical Publishing House, 1972). Translated by a team of Buddhist monks from Tibet, India, and Great Britain, *The Opening of the Wisdom Eye* is a general paraphrase of the Tibetan with long passages, absent in the original, interpolated into the text. It also does not include the author's citations of Indian sources. For these reasons, a new translation has been made.

A 1967 reprint of the original 1963 edition of the text, *Legs bshad blo gsar mid 'byed* (Dharamsala, India: Tibetan Cultural Printing Press), was used by the translators.

We wish to thank Venerable Yeshi Thupten, former abbot of the Lo-sel-ling College of Dre-bung Monastic University, for clarifying many points in *Opening the Eye of New Awareness*. We also wish to thank Gareth Sparham for typing the manuscript, Elizabeth Napper for many editorial suggestions, and Professor Richard B. Martin of the University of Virginia for bibliographic assistance.

Donald S. Lopez, Jr.
Jeffrey Hopkins

Technical Note

Occasional footnotes have been provided by the translators giving references to supplementary material and references for quotations. Transliteration of Tibetan in parentheses and in the glossary is done in accordance with a system devised by Turrell Wylie; see "A Standard System of Tibetan Transcription", *Harvard Journal of Asiatic Studies,* Vol. 22, 1959, pp.261-7. The names of Tibetan authors and orders are given in "essay phonetics" for the sake of easy pronunciation; for a discussion of the system used, see the Technical Note at the beginning of Hopkins' *Meditation on Emptiness,* pp. 19-22. For the names of Indian scholars and systems used in the body of the text, *ch, sh,* and *ṣh* are used instead of the more usual *c, ś,* and *ṣ* for the sake of easy pronunciation by non-specialists. Page numbers of the 1967 edition of the Tibetan text of *Opening the Eye of New Awareness* appear in brackets in the body of the translation.

Hope for the Future

A talk given at the Theosophical Society, Wheaton, Illinois

I will speak this evening on my usual topic – that is, about the importance of kindness and compassion. When I speak about this, I regard myself not as a Buddhist, not as the Dalai Lama, not as a Tibetan, but rather as one human being. And, I hope that you in the audience will, at this moment, think of yourselves as human beings rather than as Americans, or Westerners, or members of the Theosophical Society. These things are secondary. If from my side and from the listeners' side we interact as human beings, we will reach the basic level. If I say, "I am a monk," or "I am a Buddhist," these are, in comparison to my nature as a human being, temporary. To be a human is basic. Once you are born as a human being, that cannot change until death. Other things – educated or uneducated, rich or poor – are secondary.

At the present time we face many problems. Some are created essentially by ourselves based on divisions due to ideology, religion, race, economic status, or other factors. Therefore, the time has come when we should think on a deeper level, on the human level, and from that level we should appreciate and respect the sameness of others as human beings. We must build a closer relationship of mutual trust, understanding, respect, and help, irrespective of differences of culture, philosophy, religion, or faith.

After all, all human beings are the same – made of human flesh, bones, and blood. Also the internal feelings, the wish for happiness and not wishing for suffering are the same. Further, we all have an equal right to be happy. In other words, it is important to realize our sameness as human beings. We all belong to one human family. That we quarrel with each other is due to secondary reasons, and all of this arguing with each other, cheating each other, suppressing each other is of no use.

Unfortunately, for many centuries, bad human beings have used all sorts of methods to suppress and hurt others. Many terrible things have been done. It has meant more problems, more suffering, and more mistrust, resulting in more feelings of hatred and more divisions.

As I say again and again, the world is becoming smaller and smaller. Economically, and from many other viewpoints, the different areas of the world are becoming much closer and more heavily interdependent. Because of this, international summit meetings often take place; problems in one remote place are connected with other global crises. This situation expresses the fact that it is time, it is necessary, to think more on a human level rather than on the basis of the matters that divide us. Therefore, I am speaking to you as just a human being, and I earnestly hope that you also are listening with the thought, "I am a human being, and I am here listening to another human being."

All of us want happiness. In big cities, on farms, in remote places, throughout the countryside, people are busy and active. What is the main purpose? Everyone is trying to create happiness. To do so is right. However, it is very important to follow a right method in seeking happiness. We must keep in mind that too much involvement on a superficial level will not solve the larger problems.

There are all about us many crises, many fears. Through highly developed science and technology, we have reached an advanced level of materiai progress that is both useful and necessary. Yet, if you compare the external progress to our internal progress, it is quite clear that our internal progress is inadequate. In many countries, crises – murdering, killing, and terrorism – are chronic. People complain about the decline in morality and the rise in criminal activity. Although in external matters we are highly developed and are still progressing, at the same time it is equally important to develop and progress in terms of inner development.

In ancient times, if there was war, the effect – the amount of destruction – was limited. Today, however, because of external material progress, it is beyond imagination. Last year I visited Hiroshima. Though I knew something about the nuclear explosion there, it was a very different matter physically to visit the place, to see it with my own eyes, and to meet with people who actually suffered at that moment. I was very moved. A terrible weapon was used. Though we might regard someone as an enemy, on a deeper level an enemy is also a human being, also wants happiness, and has the right to be happy. Looking at Hiroshima and thinking about this, at that moment I became even more convinced that anger and hatred cannot solve problems.

Anger cannot be overcome by anger. If a person shows anger to you, and you also show anger, the result is disastrous. In contrast, if you control anger and show opposite attitudes – compassion, tolerance, and patience – then not only do you yourself remain in peace, but the other's anger will gradually diminish.

World problems similarly cannot be challenged by anger or hatred. Rather, they must be faced with compassion, love, and true kindness. Look at all the terrible weapons there are. Yet, the weapons themselves cannot start a war. The button to trigger them is under a human finger, which moves by thought, not under its own power. The responsibility rests in our thought.

The leaders of the great nations are talking about arms limitation and about nuclear disarmament. This is marvellous. But how is armament to be controlled? First there must be inner control; only then will real control come. Without this, even if you produce a large document with a big pen, it will not last long. If someone wants to destroy it, he can do so within seconds.

If you look deeply into all such things, the blueprint is found within – in the mind – out of which actions come. Thus, first controlling the mind is very important. I am not talking here about controlling the mind in the sense of deep meditation, but just about less anger, more respect for others' rights, more concern for other people, more clear realization of our sameness as human beings. Take the Western view of the Eastern bloc – for instance, of the Soviet Union. You must look at the Soviet Union as brothers and sisters; the people of Russia are the same as yourselves. The Russians also should look on this side as brothers and sisters. This attitude may not solve problems immediately, but we have to make the attempt, propagating this realization through magazines and through television. Rather than just advertising for money, money, money, we need something meaningful, something seriously directed towards the welfare of humankind. Not money alone. Money is necessary, but the actual purpose of money is for human beings. Sometimes we lose interest in human beings and are just concerned about money. This is not sensible.

We should spread this idea using all available media. It is not an attempt to propagate religion or a particular faith. After all, we all want happiness, and no one will argue with the fact that with anger, peace is impossible. With kindness and love, peace of mind can be achieved. No one wants anger, no one wants mental unrest, yet because of ignorance, they occur. Bad attitudes, such as depression, arise from the power of ignorance, not of their own accord.

Through anger we lose one of the best human qualities – the power of judgement. We have a good brain, which other mammals do not have, allowing us to judge what is right and what is wrong, not only in terms of today's concerns, but considering ten, twenty, or even a hundred years. Without any precognition, we can use our normal common sense to determine if something is a right or wrong method; we can decide that if we do such and such, it will lead to such and such an effect. However, once our mind is occupied by anger, we lose this power of judgement, and once lost, it is very sad. Physically you are a human being, but mentally you are incomplete. Given that we have this physical human form, we must safeguard our mental capacity for judgement. For that, we cannot take out insurance; the insurance company is within: self-discipline, self-awareness, and clear realization of the defects of anger and the positive effects of kindness. Thinking about this again and again, we can become convinced of it, and then with self-awareness, can control the mind.

For instance, at present you may be a person who gets quickly and easily irritated by small things. With clear understanding and awareness, this can be controlled. If you usually remain angry for ten minutes, try to reduce it to eight. Next week make it five minutes and the next month two. Then make it zero. That is how to develop and train our minds.

This is my feeling and also the sort of practice I myself do. It is quite clear that everyone needs peace of mind. The question, then, is how to achieve it. Through anger we cannot; through kindness, through love, through compassion, we can achieve one individual's peace of mind. The result of this is a peaceful family – no quarrels between husband and wife; you and your children will be happy; no worry about divorce. Extended to the national level, it can bring unity, harmony, and cooperation with genuine motivation. On the international level, we need mutual trust, mutual respect, frank and friendly discussion with sincere motivation, and joint effort to solve world problems. All these are possible.

First we must change within ourselves. Our national

leaders try their best to solve our problems, but when one problem is solved here, another one crops up; trying to solve that, again there is another somewhere else. The time has come to try from another angle. Of course, it is very difficult to achieve such a worldwide movement for peace of mind, but it is the only alternative. If there were another method that was more practical and easier, it would be better, but there is none. If through weapons we could achieve real lasting peace, all right. Let all factories be turned into weapon factories. Spend every dollar for that – if we achieve definite lasting peace. But this is impossible.

Weapons do not remain quiet. Once a weapon is developed, sooner or later someone will use it. Someone might feel that if you do not use it, then millions of dollars are wasted, so somehow you should use it – drop a bomb to try it out. The result is that innocent people get killed. A friend of mine told me that in Beirut there is a businessman dealing in weapons solely thinking to make money. Because of him, more of the poor people in the streets get killed every day – ten or fifteen, or a hundred. This is due to a lack of human understanding, a lack of mutual respect and trust, to not acting on a basis of kindness and love.

Therefore, making this sort of attempt at world peace through internal transformation is difficult but is the only way to achieve lasting world peace. Even if during my own lifetime it is not achieved, it is all right. More human beings will come, the next generation and the one after that, and progress can continue. I feel that despite the practical difficulties and the sense that this is almost an unrealistic view, it is worthwhile to make the attempt. Therefore, wherever I go, I express these things. I am encouraged that people from different walks of life generally receive it well.

Each of us has responsibility for all humankind. It is time for us to think of other people as true brothers and sisters and to be concerned with their welfare, with lessening their suffering. Even if you cannot sacrifice your own benefit entirely, you should not forget the concerns of others.

We should think more about the future and benefit of all humanity.

Also, if you try to subdue your selfish motives – anger, and so forth – and develop more kindness and compassion for others, ultimately you yourself will benefit more than you would otherwise. So sometimes I say that the wise selfish person should practice this way. Foolish selfish people are always thinking of themselves, and the result is negative. Wise selfish people think of others, help others as much as they can, and the result is that they too receive benefit.

This is my simple religion. There is no need for temples; no need for complicated philosophy. Our own brain, our own heart is our temple; the philosophy is kindness.

An Overview of Tibetan Buddhism

A talk at the Zen Center, Green Gulch, California. In a large hall the meditators chanted the "Heart Sūtra", after which the Dalai Lama spoke.

Dharma friends, I am truly happy to sit with you in meditation and to be here while you chant the *Heart Sūtra* in the Japanese manner, since we Tibetans also frequently recite this scripture. Over lunch, Baker Roshi explained to me your practice. It is very different, very far from ours, but just that degree of difference shows the richness and variety of Buddhism. As much as the systems appeared to be different, so much greater did my respect for Buddhism grow as I listened to him. Within having the same motivation – compassion, love, kindness, tolerance, and self-discipline – there are different philosophies and different methods, but the ultimate goal is Buddhahood in order to help all sentient beings.

Kindness, or compassion, is the basis of Buddhism. Usually we speak of Lesser and Great Vehicles, but I prefer the terms Vehicle of Hearers *(nyan thos, śrāvaka)* and Vehicle of Bodhisattvas. In the Vehicle of Hearers the main essence is not to harm others; the whole structure of that vehicle is contained within calm abiding *(zhi gnas, śamatha)* and special insight *(lhag mthong, vipaśyanā)* with ethics as their basis. Non-violence or not harming others is the root. Thus, compassion *(snying rje, karuṇā)* is the basic teaching in the Vehicle of Hearers.

In the Bodhisattva Vehicle, the essence is to serve others, to help others. Compassion has become more mature. The practice of compassion at the beginning, when your capacities to help others are still not developed, is not to harm others, but then when those capacities have developed, it is to go to others to help them. Thus, in both cases the basic teaching is compassion.

There is no question that compassion and kindness are important for those who practice religion. However, even for those who do not, these attitudes are extremely important. Even in a materialistic society, compassion and love are the basis of happiness. Whether you believe in a future life or not, whether you believe in the Buddha or not, whether you believe in the Bodhisattva path or not, love and kindness are beneficial even in worldly life. Also, love, compassion, and kindness are common to all religions – Christianity, Hinduism, Islam, Judaism, Sikhism, and so forth. Their value is clear for all – believers and non-believers.

In Buddhism, there are many explanations of techniques for developing, training in, and implementing compassion. From this viewpoint, Buddhism is very useful to society these days, particularly when there is danger of the human problems of war, unrest, violence, and terrorism. Under these circumstances, the force of compassion, the force of love and kindness, is essential. For any activity related with human society, compassion and love are vital, whether one is a politician, businessman, communist, scientist, engineer, or whatever. If such people carry out their professional work with a good motivation, that work becomes an instrument for human benefit. On the other hand, if people utilize their profession not with that motive but out of selfishness or with anger, the profession becomes distorted. Instead of bringing benefit for humankind, the knowledge gained in the profession brings more disaster for humankind. So compassion is essential. May all here practice it.

Now I will say a little about Tibetan Buddhism in general by way of the three trainings – in ethics, meditative stabilization, and wisdom. In the scriptures of the Hearer Vehicle, the training in ethics is comprised of avoiding harming others. In the Bodhisattva scriptures, the training in ethics is based on restraining selfishness. In the tantric systems, the practice of ethics is centered around restraining ordinary appearance as well as conceptions of ordinariness. Although the terminology differs from that explained earlier to me by your abbot, the overall meaning is the same.

With respect to meditative stabilization *(ting nge 'dzin, samādhi),* the process of achieving it is described in the scriptures of the Hearers, and even though in the Bodhisattva scriptures a great variety of meditative stabilizations are presented, the nature of the process is the same. However, in the tantric systems, the mode of achieving meditative stabilization becomes more profound.

The Tibetan word for concentration *(bsam gtan, dhyāna)* has just the same meaning as "zen". To describe briefly how it is achieved, when we meditate, first of all there is an object of observation that is either an external object or the mind itself. In the latter case, when the mind itself is taken as the object of observation, the practice is more profound.

In terms of posture, sit in either the full or half cross-legged posture with the hands in the position of meditative equipoise, the left hand below the right and the two thumbs touching, making a triangle the base of which is about four finger widths below the navel. The cushion is such that your rear is higher, the effect being that no matter how much meditative stabilization is cultivated you do not become tired. The backbone is to be straightened like an arrow; the neck is to be bent just a little downward; aim your eyes over the nose to the front; attach the tongue to the roof of the mouth; leave your lips and teeth as usual, and leave your arms a little loose, not forcing them against the body.

If your mind is involved with desire or hatred, it is necessary first to engage in a technique to loosen from it. Meditation on the inhalation and exhalation of the breath up to a count of twenty-one is the prime means for doing so. Since the mind cannot have two modes of apprehension simultaneously, this meditation causes the former conceptuality to fade. Then, it is necessary to form a virtuous motivation of compassion and altruism, wishing to help others.

Conventional and ultimate modes of being of the mind are set forth; here you are settling first the conventional status of the mind. For that, do not let your mind think about what has happened in the past, nor let it chase after things that might happen in the future; rather, leave the mind vivid, without any constructions, just as it is. When you remain this way, you understand that the mind, like a mirror, is such that any object, any conception, is capable of appearing under certain circumstances, like reflections, and that the entity of the mind has a nature of mere luminosity and knowing, of mere experience. When you identify the nature of the mind as mere luminosity and knowing, hold on to that experiential factor – the mere luminosity and knowingness – and stay with it.

That is how to use the mind itself as an object of observation in the process of achieving meditative stabilization. If, rather than the mind, you use an external object of observation such as the body of Mañjushrī, first take a good look at a well-designed image of Mañjushrī and visualize it mentally, causing an internal image of it to appear to the mind.

Whether the object of observation is internal – the mind – or external, such as a Buddha's body, once you mentally locate it, techniques are needed to cause the mind to remain vividly on that object. Since sound is the thorn preventing concentration, initially it is very important to stay in a quiet place such as this meditation center. Also, factors of both stability and clarity are needed with respect to the object. What prevents the factor of stability is the mind's scattering, or excitement. When the mind does not stay on the object but becomes distracted, scattered, or excited, there is a coarse version of excitement in which the object of observation is lost, but there are also subtler forms in which, even if the object of observation is not lost, a corner of the mind is thinking about something else. You need to identify such scattering and excitement and, through mindfulness, not let the mind come under their influence.

The initial obstacle to the factor of clarity is lethargy, a heaviness of mind and body. Lethargy also can serve as a cause of laxity, which prevents clarity. Again, there are two types of laxity, coarse and subtle. In coarse laxity the mind sinks, and the object of observation fades and is lost. In subtle laxity, even if the object is not lost, the clarity of the object and the clarity of the mind diminish, the mind's factor of intensity having weakened; here, the mind is too loose.

As an antidote to becoming scattered or excited, you need to lower the mode of apprehension of the mind. Similarly, when you have laxity, it is necessary to heighten the mode of apprehension. A moderate mode of apprehension of the mind is needed – lowering or loosening it when there is danger of excitement and heightening it when there is danger of laxity.

Thus, the force behind developing meditative stabilization is mindfulness, the factor of holding on to, and not allowing distraction from, an object with which you have become familiar. What supports this process is introspection that inspects from time to time to see whether laxity or excitement have arisen. It is said that when the continuum of holding the object of observation is sustained through mindfulness and introspection and when one has the concordant circumstances of good merit and so forth, it is possible to achieve meditative stabilization within six months.

As you develop meditative stabilization, your mind passes through nine stages. In brief, initially you must forcibly put the mind on the object of observation with great exertion; then you interruptedly engage the object without such great exertion, then more relaxedly engage it without interruption, and finally spontaneously stay on the object without any of the exertion required for applying the antidotes to laxity and excitement. If you are able to stay for four hours vividly and continuously on the object of observation without exertion, you have achieved the factor of firm stability of mind. Unfavorable conditions of body and mind that would make them unserviceable in a virtuous direction are removed in that the winds, or energies, that support body and mind are removed, and a bliss of physical and mental pliancy in which body and mind are serviceable in virtue is attained. At that point, you have achieved the meditative stabilization of calm abiding. [For a more detailed presentation, see Chapter 5.]

Although this type of meditative stabilization is indispensable for achieving the higher paths, its entity itself is shared with Hindu and other non-Buddhist systems. In the non-Buddhist Forder *(mu stegs pa, tīrthika)* systems, one actualizes this meditative stabilization of calm abiding, called the "not unable" *(mi lcog med, anāgamya),* which is a preparation for the first concentration and then through six mental contemplations achieves the first concentration, the second, third, and fourth and then the four formless absorptions, of limitless space, limitless consciousness, nothingness, and the peak of cyclic existence – levels of increasingly subtle meditative stabilization. However, in the Buddhist systems of sūtra and especially of tantra, it is explained that it is sufficient to achieve merely this "not unable" mental contemplation that is a preparation for the first concentration, the higher levels of concentration not being necessary.

What is the purpose in achieving such meditative stabilization? It is not just for the sake of gaining a mind of a higher level such as the first concentration, *temporarily* suppressing the manifest coarse afflictions through viewing the lower level as gross and the higher level as peaceful; it is not just for the sake of proceeding in the manner of a mundane path.

Rather, the purpose of meditative stabilization is to serve as a basis for achieving the supramundane special insight realizing selflessness through which the afflictions can be removed completely and forever.

To generate the wisdom realizing selflessness in your continuum, it is necessary first to realize the meaning of emptiness, selflessness. Whereas "meditating on faith" means that faith is cultivated in the sense of causing the mind to be generated into the entity of a faith consciousness, "meditating on selflessness" means to take selflessness, or emptiness, as an object of meditation, as the object of the mode of apprehension of your mind. To do that, it is necessary to know what selflessness, emptiness, is.

As is clear in Nāgārjuna's *Fundamental Treatise on the Middle Way (dbu ma'i bstan gcos, madhyamakaśāstra)*, phenomena are not said to be empty because of being unable to perform functions; rather, all phenomena are empty because of being dependent-arisings. Nāgārjuna did not give as the reason why phenomena are empty that they are unable to perform functions but, instead, gave as the reason the fact that they are dependent-arisings. From this, it can be understood that the meaning of emptiness is the meaning of dependent-arising.

Since things are dependent-arisings, are dependently established, there is nothing that is established independently. Dependent and independent are explicitly mutually exclusive, a dichotomy; thus, once things are dependently established, they are definitely not independent. Independence or non-dependence on others – establishment under the object's own power – is called "self"; because it does not exist, we speak of selflessness.

According to the Consequence School *(thal 'gyur pa, prāsaṅgika)*, which embodies Nāgārjuna's thought exactly as it is, there are two types of selflessness: of persons and of other phenomena. These are divided only by way of the substrata – persons and other phenomena – which are without self, or independent existence, and not by way of a difference in the emptiness of these two.

To ascertain the meaning of selflessness, in general you must engage in analytical meditation, reflectively analyzing with reasoning. This is why in Nāgārjuna's *Fundamental Treatise on the Middle Way* many reasonings are presented, all for the sake of proving from many viewpoints that all phenomena are empty of being established under their own power, empty of inherent existence. The "Questions of Kāshyapa Chapter" *('os srung gi le'u, kāśyapaparivarta)* of the *Pile of Jewels Sūtra (dkon btsegs, ratnakūṭa),* in the context of presenting the three doors of liberation, says that, in brief, forms are not empty *because* of emptiness, forms themselves are empty. Therefore, emptiness does not mean that a phenomenon is empty of being some other object but that it itself is empty of its own inherent existence. Thus, it is not an other-emptiness but a self-emptiness in that objects are empty of their *own* intrinsic establishment.

Similarly, the *Heart Sūtra* says, "Form is emptiness; emptiness is form." Taking form as an example, that form is emptiness means that the final nature of forms is their natural voidness of inherent existence. Because forms are dependent-arisings, they are empty of an independent self-powered entity.

That emptiness is form means that this natural voidness of inherent existence – this final nature, emptiness, which is the absence of a basic self-powered principle of these things that exist in the manner of depending on other factors – makes possible the forms that are its sport or are established from it in dependence upon conditions. Since forms are those that are empty of true establishment – since forms are the bases of emptiness – emptiness is form; forms appear as like reflections of emptiness.

This final nature of forms is their absence of not depending on other factors; forms themselves are not their own final nature but are empty of being their own final nature. Thus forms are the sport of emptiness. Like the two sides of the hand, when looked at from this side, there is the emptiness of inherent existence, the final nature, but when looked at from the other side, there is the appearance that is the substratum of emptiness. They are one entity. Therefore, form is emptiness, and emptiness is form.

Contemplating the meaning of emptiness in this way, you gradually make progress over the paths. The progression is indicated in the mantra in the *Heart Sūtra: gate gate pāragate pārasaṃgate bodhi svāhā* [Proceed, proceed, proceed beyond, thoroughly proceed beyond, be founded in enlightenment]. The first *gate* refers to the path of accumulation; the second, to the path of preparation. Over these two periods you ascertain emptiness in the manner of dualistic appearance of the wisdom consciousness and the emptiness being realized. Then, "proceed beyond" indicates passing beyond the mundane level to the supramundane level of the path of seeing in which dualistic appearance has vanished. "Thoroughly proceed beyond" refers to the path of meditation during which you familiarize yourself again and again with the emptiness that was first directly seen on the path of seeing. Through it, you finally pass beyond cyclic existence to the level of enlightenment *(bodhi)* – a state of being a source of help and happiness for all sentient beings.

This is a brief explanation of emptiness, the object with respect to which a practitioner first develops the wisdom arisen from hearing, then ascertains with the wisdom arisen from thinking, and finally, in dependence upon meditation on it, proceeds over the stages of the path.

The above has been an explanation of the three trainings of ethics, meditative stabilization, and wisdom in the sūtra system. In Highest Yoga Tantra, meditation on emptiness is done mainly by way of stabilizing meditation rather than with analytical meditation. In connection with this there are many techniques involving focusing on important places in the body, the four or six channel centers *('khor lo, cakra)* and so forth.

In this way, a system of practice is explained in which one person simultaneously practices all three vehicles – externally abiding in the discipline of individual liberation, internally practicing the altruistic intention to become enlightened, and secretly supplementing these with secret mantra [tantra]. That is a brief explanation of the situation in Tibetan Buddhism.

I have great admiration for your system of practice, too. When we strive for inner development, great achievement is very difficult, almost impossible, within a short period. So, when beginning to practice, we should not expect too much. With a mental attitude of patience and strong determination, as time passes year by year, inner progress will develop. As one Tibetan lama said, "Suddenly looking at it, it may seem as if it is impossible for someone like oneself to be able to do these things. However, compounded phenomena do not remain as they are; they change with conditions. If you do not become discouraged and keep working at it, something that you think could not be produced in a hundred years is one day produced." Therefore, for us who supposedly practice these things, will-power and determination are essential. Also, while we practice inner development, daily conduct according to moral principles is very important for the benefit of both ourselves and society.

If we who are supposed to be practicing Buddhist doctrines of kindness and so forth lead a good and reasonable life, it is a demonstration, an example, for others to help them realize the value of Buddhism. People who pretend to practice a system but whose conduct and way of life are not good and reasonable not only accumulate non-virtue themselves but also harm the teaching in general. Therefore, it is important to be conscientious. This is my appeal.

Thank you. I have been very happy here. As you were ringing the bell this morning, I had a sense of being at my own monastery in Tibet. I was very, very happy remembering the same time in Tibet when it was still dark before dawn and the bell was ringing – feeling a little sleepy.

Opening the Eye of New Awareness

1 *The Need for Religious Practice*

Homage to the final exalted wisdom thoroughly differentiating phenomena.

At this time of the twentieth century, an era of chemicals and weaponry – during the Phase of Ethics among the ten periods of five hundred years[1] in the teaching of the Fourth Leader, the Teacher [Shākyamuni Buddha][2] – external material culture has and is continuing to develop and expand. At the same time, there is a vital need for similar development and expansion of inner awareness and attitude.

In the Buddhist way, internal culture is achieved through thought and meditation, and for that it is necessary to know how to think and how to meditate. Therefore, in accordance with the merit of those beings who do not have the leisure to study the great texts, profound and full of impact, I write this *Opening the Eye of New Awareness,* a treatise of few words, primarily for easy comprehension, expanding the illumination of the wisdom that thoroughly differentiates phenomena.

All beings are equal in that they want happiness and do not want suffering. This does not apply merely to us humans of brighter intelligence; all, even dumb and obscured creatures, from the tiniest insect on up, only want happiness and do not want even small suffering. [2] Therefore, everyone, ourselves and others, must find a method to cause happiness to arise and to keep suffering from arising. Without it, it is impossible for happiness to arise and for suffering to be eliminated merely by waiting with the great hope, "How nice it would be if I had happiness and did not have suffering!" Consequently, we must establish the causes from which happiness arises and abandon the bases of the arising of suffering.

The means for establishing the causes of benefit and happiness and for abandoning harm and suffering cannot be gained by any other way as fully and completely as they are through religious practice. Through religious practice we are able to bring about happiness and alleviate suffering in this and many future lifetimes – this life, the next life, the life after that, and so forth. [3]

Even in the case of this lifetime, nothing surpasses religious practice for bringing about happiness and abandoning suffering. For example, in cases of physical illness there is a very great difference between those who have and those who have not understood the essential meaning of religion in terms of the degree of their mental and physical suffering and their ability to alleviate that suffering. A person who has not understood the essentials of religious practice and who does not have any of the ambrosia of the magnificent impact of such practice has, in addition to strong feelings of physical sickness, the great suffering of not being able mentally to bear that illness; he or she is troubled by both physical and mental suffering with no opportunity for happiness.

However, if a person has understood the essential points of religious practice, he or she voluntarily accepts suffering with the thought, for example, that it is the fruit of ill deeds accumulated in the past and, seeing that suffering is the nature of cyclic existence, wishes to take responsibility for previous actions. As a result, mental suffering does not arise, and because it does not arise, the pain can be alleviated when the power of internal thought suppresses the external suffering of physical sickness. [4] The reason for this is that between body and mind, the mind is, so to speak, the prime controller of the body, and the body is as if under the control of the mind. Therefore, mental feelings of pleasure and pain are stronger [than those of the body].

Similarly, some people who desire the happiness of riches accumulate and guard their wealth, incurring great physical and mental fatigue. They suffer initially from the inability to amass as much wealth as they had hoped for. Even after gaining some wealth, they suffer in the meantime from the inability to protect it from being stolen by others, its loss and destruction, its being squandered, and the like. In the end, there is the suffering that no matter what they do their wealth becomes the property of others and they themselves must part from it forever. All such sufferings related with wealth and resources result from not having understood the essential topics of religious practice. When those are understood, one sees that all wealth is as essenceless as the dew on the tip of a blade of grass [which evaporates quickly at dawn] and, consequently, one does not undergo any of the sufferings that are associated with the wearying accumulation and guarding of wealth and [the suffering of] separating from it against one's wish. [5]

In the same way, when unpleasant words of open abuse, covert blame, slander, and so forth are spoken by others about oneself, there arises a suffering like being pierced in the heart with a thorn. However, if we understand the essential topics of religious practice, we see that all of these are essenceless, like an echo, and even slight suffering does not arise, as if mindless matter had been abused.

Similarly, in this lifetime, the suffering of not subduing enemies, the suffering of not keeping friends, the suffering of others winning and oneself losing – in short, all the hopes and fears based on gain and loss, happiness and unhappiness, all physical and mental pain whatsoever – and not only those, the arising of terrifying warfare due to mutual hostility and discord between nations, destroying the happiness of countless beings with not even the name "happiness" remaining such that suffering roils like turbulent water – in brief, the great and small sufferings that occur in this life are due to not understanding religious practice or, although understanding it, not putting it to use. [6]

If religion is understood and practiced, all these sufferings can be destroyed. Why? All such difficulties arise only in dependence on such things as pride, miserliness, jealousy, and the three – desire, hatred, and obscuration.

By pacifying and overcoming these faults [which are mainly mental] through the power of religious practice, one achieves knowledge of contentment as well as self-concern, concern for others' opinion, and conscientiousness; body and mind remain constantly in pleasant tranquility, whereby unbearable suffering does not arise. Therefore, if we want happiness and pleasure in this life and do not want suffering, it is very important to understand the essential topics of religion and then implement them in practice.

Doing so, however, we should not be satisfied merely with happiness in this life. No matter how great the happiness of this life may be, it lasts only until death – not more than a hundred years, since no one lives much longer than that. [7] Future lives are the journey of greater length, and thus we must secure that long-range interest; we must work for means of gaining happiness and alleviating suffering in future lifetimes. Furthermore, there is absolutely no way to achieve such happiness through techniques other than religious practice.

REBIRTH

Here in the context of explaining the need to accomplish the purposes of future births, let us consider the opinions of certain people who do not know about the doctrine of rebirth or who know a little about it but do not fully comprehend the reasons for it. It might occur to them that the present mind depends exclusively on the body and that because they do not directly witness former and future lifetimes, they do not exist. Their idea is that if something exists it must be seen directly.

Or, they think that the mind is produced in dependence on the body, the body arises in dependence on the four great elements [earth, water, fire, and wind], and therefore former lifetimes do not exist; at death the body turns into the four elements and the mind turns into space, like a disappearing rainbow. [8] Hence, they conclude that it cannot be said that there are subsequent lifetimes.

Among those who think that mental awareness depends on the body, there are some who think the mind is of the nature of the body, like beer and its capacity to intoxicate; others think that mind is an effect of the body, like a lamp and its light; and still others think that the mind is a quality of the body, like a wall and a mural on it. Thus, they basically think that a mind that was just produced in this life need not have been produced from an earlier mind of similar type but rather is produced from mindless elements, which are of dissimilar type, as is the case, for example, with the power of intoxication from beer or fire from a magnifying glass – in other words, the arising of an effect that does not accord with its cause.

Similarly, some mistaken logicians observe that there is no one who makes peas round, sharpens thorns, or colors the eyes of a peacock's feathers. They observe that there are uncharitable misers who become wealthy, murderers who live long lives and so forth, and, therefore, they assert with bogus reasons that there is no such thing as the cause and effect of actions *(las, karma)* [carrying over from one lifetime to another]. [9] There are also some with meditative absorption *(snyoms 'jug, samāpatti)* who use clairvoyance to see that a certain person who was miserly in a former life is born into a wealthy home in the next life and, due to this, assert that although there are former and later lives, there is no cause and effect of actions. Also, there are some who achieve a concentration *(bsam gtan, dhyāna)* or formless absorption *(gzugs med kyi snyoms 'jug, ārūpyasamāpatti)* through meditative stabilization *(ting nge 'dzin, samādhi)* and believe that they have achieved liberation *(thar pa, mokṣa)*. When they fall from that state and see that they must again take rebirth, they conclude that liberation does not exist and hence assert that it does not.

Though there are a variety of such assertions, former and later lifetimes do exist, and the reason is this: Even now as adults we remember states of mind from last year, the year before that, and so forth back to childhood. Hence, it is established in our own direct experience that there existed a mind that was the earlier continuum of the present mind as an adult. In the same way, the beginning of consciousness in this life was also not produced causelessly, nor was it produced by something permanent, nor was it produced from mindless matter. [10] If it were, matter would be a substantial cause of dissimilar type. Hence, it definitely must have been produced from a substantial cause of similar type.

With regard to how the type [of effect] is similar [to the cause] in this case, the mind [of the new life] itself is a sentience or awareness that is a factor of luminosity and knowing. It is, therefore, preceded by a similar factor of luminosity and knowing. That former mind is not suitable to be anything but a mind produced in an earlier lifetime; otherwise, if only the physical elements acted as the substantial cause of the mind, there would be faults such as that a corpse would have consciousness and that when the body is enhanced or deteriorates, consciousness would necessarily be enhanced or deteriorate.

Something suitable to become a mental entity is called the substantial cause of the mind. The physical body acts merely as a cooperative condition for the slight amplification or constriction of the mind; it in no way acts as the substantial cause of mind. Hence, there is utterly no such thing as non-mind becoming mind or mind becoming non-mind. [11]

Regarding this, some, [who hold that transformation of non-mind into mind can occur, attempt] to prove the existence of such transformation with the example of the changes of certain external things [such as wood becoming fire, wood becoming stone (petrified wood), etc.]. However, change in the formless mind is different from change in physical things and [there is no way that insentient matter can turn into] formless sentience and awareness just as, for example, something that is not space does not become space and space itself does not become non-space.

Hence, concerning the present physical body and non-physical mind, the body is established through the parents' semen and blood [i.e., ovum] acting as the substantial cause, but it is impossible for the parents' minds ever to act as the substantial cause of the mind. This can be known, for example, by the fact that intelligent parents skilled in fields of knowledge can have stupid children.

No factor of the parents' body or mind becomes the mind of the child of this life. The actual fact is this: The mind that comes from the former life acts as the substantial cause of the mind of the present life, and the present parents' semen and blood serve as the substantial cause of the body. [12] The relationship of those two [child and parents] is established by an action *(las, karma)* from a former lifetime. Consequently, newborn children, calves, and so forth eat food and suckle as soon as they are born without having to learn. This is due to the power of having become accustomed to eating food, being desirous, being hateful, and so forth in their previous lifetimes. Their engagement in these activities is caused by the presence of earlier predispositions *(bag chags, vāsanā)* in the mind. The master Matṛcheta's [Āryaśūra] *Garland of Birth Stories (skyes rabs kyi rgyud, jātakamālā)* (XXIX. 12-13) says:

> That one just born,
> Its mind without strength,
> With senses dull,
> Seeks breasts to suck and food to eat,
> Untaught by anyone,
> Is clearly due to being used to
> these in other lives.[3] [13]

It is also unsuitable to think that former and later lives do not exist because they are not directly perceived; one cannot posit something as non-existent simply because one has not seen it. There are many internal and external phenomena newly seen or heard through modern technology that were not heard or seen by our ancestors.

Moreover, [knowledge of] former and later lifetimes [arises] in those who have reached a high level of meditative stabilization due to the power of religious meditation. Furthermore, there are many persons who remember the circumstances of former lifetimes due to predisposing tendencies from the past. There is also the account of a Buddhist scholar in India who, after debating with a Nihilist, wanted his opponent to have direct knowledge of former and later lifetimes and thus, with the king and others as witnesses, died and was reborn as the master Chandragomin.[4] In Tibet as well, there have been many persons who remembered their former lives, recognizing persons, possessions, and so forth of the earlier lifetime and relating events of the past. [14]

Therefore, since we certainly have future lives, we definitely must do something about them. The way to do so is this: having cultivated a good mind, we must strive at a means to eliminate all faults and cause all good qualities to arise. The method is either to cultivate a good path over successive lifetimes or to achieve a path that has the capacity to sever the continuum of cyclic existence in this very lifetime, through relying on a profound technique, so that we do not have to die and be reborn in cyclic existence *('khor ba, saṃsāra)*.

2 *The Two Truths*

In order to achieve such liberation, one must know presentations of how to ascertain the basis – the two truths [conventional truths and ultimate truths], how to practice the path – method and wisdom – and, in dependence on that, how to achieve the goal – the two Buddha Bodies [Form Body and Truth Body]. [15] First, what is the presentation of the basis that is to be ascertained, the two truths?

The *Meeting of Father and Son Sūtra (yab sras mjal ba'i mdo, pitāputrasamāgamasūtra)* says:[5]

> The Knower of the World, without listening to others,
> Taught in terms of just these two truths:
> The conventional and the ultimate.
> There is no third truth.

Similarly, Nāgārjuna's *Fundamental Treatise on the Middle Way Called "Wisdom" (dbu ma rtsa ba'i tshig le'ur byas pa shes rab ces bya ba, prajñānāmamūlamadhyamakakārikā,* XXIV. 8a) also says:[6]

> Doctrines taught by Buddhas
> Rely completely on the two truths.

The basis of the division [into the two truths] is objects of knowledge *(shes bya, jñeya)*. Objects of knowledge are twofold: conventional truths *(kun rdzob bden pa, saṃvṛtisatya)* and ultimate truths *(don dam bden pa, paramārthasatya)*.

When something is established to be an ultimate truth, the possibility of its being a conventional truth is eliminated, and when something is established to be a conventional truth, the possibility of its being an ultimate truth is eliminated. [16] Therefore, the two truths are mutually exclusive. Also, if either of the two truths did not exist, all objects of knowledge would not be encompassed, and because there is no such thing as a third truth that is neither of these two, their enumeration eliminates a third category.

If the two truths were [totally] different in the sense of not being even merely the same entity, there would be four faults:

1 The fault would be incurred that the absence of true existence of a form would not be the mode of existence of a form.
2 The fault would be incurred that even though one realized the absence of true existence of a form, this would not overcome the apprehension of signs [of true existence] of a form.
3 The fault would be incurred that it would be pointless for yogis to cultivate higher paths.
4 The fault would be incurred that even a Buddha would not have abandoned the fetters of the apprehension of signs [of true existence] and all the stains of assuming bad states.

If the two truths were the same in that they could not be distinguished as separate even in terms of mere isolates *(ldog pa, vyatireka)* [i.e., conceptually isolatable factors], there would be four faults:

1 The fault would be incurred that just as actions and afflictions, which are conventionalities having a mistaken nature, are abandoned, so ultimate reality also would be abandoned. [17]

2 The fault would be incurred that the ultimate would have many different aspects just as the conventional does.
3 The fault would be incurred that even common beings would directly realize the ultimate.
4 The fault would be incurred that the afflictive emotions of desire and so forth would be produced upon observing ultimate reality.[7]

Therefore, the two truths are the same entity but different isolates [i.e., conceptually isolatable factors].

ULTIMATE TRUTHS

An ultimate truth is the object explicitly found by a reasoning consciousness analyzing the ultimate. A conventional awareness is an awareness that is involved with [objects of] worldly terminology or conventions; an object explicitly found by that [awareness] is a conventional truth.

In Sanskrit, ultimate truth is *paramārtha-satya*. *Parama* is used for "highest", "supreme", etc. *Artha* is used for "object". *Satya* is used for "truth", "permanent", etc. In this context, *artha* does not refer to welfare or purpose as in the case of speaking of one's own welfare and the welfare of others; [18] it means "object" because it is the object known, the object analyzed, and the object found by the highest exalted wisdom. It is such an object, and because it is the *supreme* and *ultimate* of objects, it is the ultimate object. It is a truth because its mode of appearance and mode of being are not discordant, as is the case with false conventionalities; rather, its mode of appearance and mode of being agree. [Therefore] it is called a truth that is the ultimate object, an ultimate truth.

When ultimate truths are divided, there are two: selflessnesses of persons *(gang zag gi bdag med, pudgalanairātmya)* and selflessnesses of phenomena *(chos kyi bdag med, dharmanairātmya)*. The master Chandrakīrti's *Supplement to* [*Nāgārjuna's*] *"Treatise on the Middle Way" (dbu ma la 'jug pa, madhyamakāvatāra,* VI.179–180) says:[8]

In order to release transmigrators [from the afflictive obstructions and the obstructions to omniscience],[9]
This selflessness was described as of two types through a division into phenomena and persons.
Therefore, the Teacher spoke to disciples frequently
Of these [two selflessnesses][10] extensively in many ways.

Having explained sixteen emptinesses
In the elaborate way, he again
Explained four in the brief way.
These also are described [11] in the Great Vehicle. [19]

When further divided, there are four emptinesses: the emptiness of functioning things, the emptiness of non-functioning things, the emptiness of the nature [i.e., of the emptinesses that are the nature of phenomena], and the emptiness of an entity [that is the object of the supramundane exalted wisdom that is] other [than the world].[12] Also, there are the sixteen emptinesses, such as the emptiness of the internal; the eighteen emptinesses; the twenty emptinesses; etc.

CONVENTIONAL TRUTHS

Conventional truths refer to all the varieties of phenomena that are not emptinesses. When they are divided extensively, there are the five aggregates *(phung po, skandha),* the twelve sources *(skye mched, āyatana),* the eighteen constituents *(khams, dhātu),* and so forth. Vasubandhu's *Treasury of Knowledge (chos mngon pa'i mdzod, abhidharmakośa,* I.20a) says:[13]

Heap, door of production, and type
Are the meaning of aggregate, source, and constituent.

Five Aggregates

From among the five aggregates *(phung po, skandha),* the first, the form *(gzugs, rūpa)* aggregate, is the five internal physical sense powers *(dbang po, indriya)* such as the eye sense, the five external forms – forms, sounds, odors, tastes, and objects of touch – making ten, and non-revelatory forms *(rnam par rig byed ma yin pa'i gzugs, avijñaptirūpa)*, making eleven. [20]

The second is the feeling *(tshor ba, vedanā)* aggregate, which is feelings of pleasure, pain, and neutrality.

The third, the discrimination *('du shes, saṃjñā)* aggregate, is of two types: conceptual and non-conceptual, each of which also has three types: small, vast, and limitless.[14]

Regarding the fourth aggregate, compositional factors *('du byed, saṃskāra)*, the associated compositional factor aggregate is all mental factors *(sems byung, caitta)* with the exception of feeling and discrimination. The non-associated compositional factor aggregate is the fourteen non-associated factors.[15]

The fifth aggregate, consciousness *(rnam shes, vijñāna)*, refers to the six consciousnesses from the eye consciousness through the mental consciousness.

Twelve Sources

Regarding the twelve sources *(skye mched, āyatana)*, the six internal sources [of consciousness] are the eye, ear, nose, tongue, body, and mental sense powers. The six external sources [of consciousness or fields of consciousness] are the form-source, sound-source, odor-source, taste-source, object-of-touch-source, and phenomenon-source. [21]

Eye sense power *(mig gi dbang po, cakṣurindriya)* and eye-source *(mig gi skye mched, cakṣurāyatana)* are synonyms, but form-source *(gzugs kyi skye mched, rupāyatana)* and form *(gzugs, rūpa)* are not synonymous. A form-source is only the object apprehended by an eye consciousness and thus [must be] colors and shapes [whereas form also includes sounds, odors, tastes, and objects of touch].

Sound, sound-source, and object of hearing by an ear consciousness are synonyms. The same is true for odors, tastes, and objects of touch [that is, odor, odor-source, and object of apprehension by a nose consciousness are synonyms, etc.] The first five of the external and internal sources are physical.

Because mind *(sems, citta)*, sentience *(yid, manas)*, and main consciousness *(rnam shes, vijñāna)* are synonyms, all main minds, such as a main eye consciousness, are mind-sources. Uncompounded phenomena such as space and emptiness are phenomena-sources.

Eighteen Constituents

The eighteen constituents *(khams, dhātu)* are:

1 the six constituents that are sense powers – the supports – the eye, ear, nose, tongue, body, and mental sense powers.
2 the six consciousness constituents – the supported – the eye, ear, nose, tongue, body, and mental consciousnesses.
3 the six constituents that are objects – the observed objects – forms, sounds, odors, tastes, objects-of-touch, and other phenomena.

In summary, all compounded phenomena are included in the five aggregates, and all objects of knowledge are included in the twelve sources as well as in the eighteen constituents. [22] Therefore, all the phenomena of the two truths are included in the twelve sources and eighteen constituents. When constituents are further divided, there are the sixty-two and so forth.

THE PURPOSE OF DELINEATING PHENOMENA

In brief, since their entities, functions, divisions, whether or not they are objects to be abandoned, and so forth must be known, one should become skilled in the six topics to be skilled in [the aggregates, sources, constituents, the twelve branches of dependent arising, the sources and non-sources of happiness and suffering, and the four truths], thereby coming to know what is to be adopted and discarded and, through that, achieving the bliss of liberation, the state of permanent separation from all suffering.

Because our minds and mental factors are under the influence of the afflictive emotions *(nyon mongs, kleśa),* we incessantly experience this wheel of suffering in cyclic existence, and thus when those afflictive emotions are abandoned, liberation is attained. Therefore, it is essential that the afflictive emotions, such as desire, be tamed. The Supramundane Victorious Buddha set forth eighty-four thousand bundles of doctrine as means for taming them. [23]

3 *How the Buddha's Pronouncements are Included in the Three Scriptural Collections*

THREE SCRIPTURAL COLLECTIONS

The eighty-four thousand collections of doctrine are included in the twelve branches of scripture,[16] which in turn are included in the three scriptural collections *(sde snod, piṭaka):* sets of discourses *(mdo sde, sutrānta),* discipline *('dul ba, vinaya),* and manifest knowledge *(chos mngon pa, abhidharma).* The Superior Maitreya's *Ornament for the Great Vehicle Sūtras (theg pa chen po'i mdo sde rgyan, mahāyānasūtrālaṃkāra)* (XI.1) says:[17]

> The scriptural collections are either three or two.
> Nine reasons are asserted for including [them in three].

There are nine reasons for positing three scriptural collections: three reasons in terms of objects of abandonment, three reasons in terms of trainings, and three reasons in terms of objects to be known.

Three Scriptural Collections And Three Objects of Abandonment

The three objects of abandonment are the secondary afflictions of (1) doubt, (2) extreme behaviour, and (3) holding one's own view to be supreme. The antidote to secondary afflictions of doubt is the scriptural collection of the sets of discourses; the antidote to secondary afflictions of extreme behaviour is the scriptural collection of discipline, and the antidote to the secondary affliction of holding one's own [mistaken or low] view to be supreme is the scriptural collection of manifest knowledge. [24]

In the scriptural collection of the sets of discourses, the aggregates, constituents, sources, dependent arising, the four truths, the grounds *(sa, bhūmi),* the perfections, and so forth are delineated well, primarily in the context of the training in meditative stabilization. Thus, the scriptural collection of the sets of discourses was set forth as an antidote to the secondary affliction of doubt because it removes doubts – qualms in two directions – concerning the specific and general characteristics of those categories of objects of knowledge.

In the scriptural collection of the discipline, engagement in all unseemly faults such as attachment to internal desires for impure behaviour, etc., and external desires for good food, clothing, residence, furnishings, etc. are prohibited, thereby [avoiding] the extreme of indulgent desires. Also, the use of even very good food, clothing, residence, and so forth is allowed for those who have pure ethics of renunciation, who need not acquire possessions and so forth through hardship and toil, and who, when making use of them, have antidotes capable of stopping strong attachment. [25] Thereby, the extreme of fatiguing and wearying asceticism [is avoided. In this way] the scriptural collection of discipline was set forth as an antidote to the secondary afflictions of the two extremes of behaviour in that it teaches antidotes to the extremes of indulgent desire and of fatiguing asceticism.

To summarize: If one makes use of good food, clothing, residence, and furnishings without producing afflictions such as attachment, pride, and arrogance, it is seemly behavior and, therefore, was permitted by the Buddha. Even though one has mediocre food and used clothing, if attachment and so forth to them increase, it is unseemly behavior and, therefore, was not permitted by the Buddha. Thus the important points in permission and prohibition are just the decrease and increase of internal afflictions such as desire; external factors are not of prime importance.

In the scriptural collection of manifest knowledge, the specific characteristics of phenomena and their general characteristics such as impermanence, suffering, and selflessness are clearly and unerringly delineated. [26] If one becomes immersed in these through hearing and thinking about them, (1) the afflictions of mistaken views conceiving [what is unclean, painful, impermanent, and selfless] to be pure, pleasant, permanent, and having a self are extinguished of their own accord, as are (2) ethics motivated by those [misconceptions], and (3) conceptions of bad modes of behavior to be good. For that reason, the scriptural collection of manifest knowledge was set forth as the antidote for conceiving one's own [mistaken] view to be supreme.

Three Scriptural Collections And Three Trainings

The second set of three reasons for positing the scriptural collections as three is as follows. The scriptural collection of the sets of discourses is posited from the viewpoint of taking the three trainings as its subject matter. The scriptural collection of discipline is posited for the purpose of achieving the trainings in ethics and in meditative stabilization, and the scriptural collection of manifest knowledge is posited for the purpose of achieving the training in wisdom. The three scriptural collections are posited with those three reasons.

Furthermore, regarding the manner in which the scriptural collection of the sets of discourses takes the three trainings as its subject matter, from the viewpoint of the Lesser Vehicle, it [teaches] the ethics of personal restraint with the vows of individual liberation, of completely pure spheres of activity and duties, and of viewing even the slightest unseemliness with concern. [27] It teaches the meditative stabilizations of the concentrations and formless absorptions in the Lesser Vehicle mode, and it teaches the training in wisdom – the special insight knowing the four truths just as they are – from the viewpoint of the Lesser Vehicle. From the viewpoint of the Great Vehicle, it teaches the training in ethics, such as the restraint of ill-deeds, etc., the training in meditative stabilizations, such as the "sky-treasury", "heroic travel", etc., and it teaches the training in wisdom – the non-conceptual exalted wisdom realizing the ultimate mode of being. Thus the scriptural collection of the sets of discourses takes all three trainings of the higher and lower vehicles as its subject matter.

Regarding the way in which the scriptural collection of discipline provides training in both ethics and meditative stabilization, it unerringly teaches the things to be adopted and discarded, engaged in and opposed, and thereby explicitly purifies ethics. When ethics are purified in that way, mental pangs and regret [for misdeeds] disappear, and when those are absent, one attains physical lightness or pliancy. [28] Consequently, mental joy and bliss increase, through the power of which the mind comes to abide one-pointedly. Thereby, both ethics and meditative stabilization are established through the scriptural collection of discipline.

Regarding the way in which the training in wisdom is established through the scriptural collection of knowledge, because [that scriptural collection] delineates and differentiates well the characteristics of phenomena, the wisdom that unerringly knows the characteristics of phenomena is produced by listening to the scriptural collection of knowledge. Through that, the training in higher wisdom is established and manifestly attained.

Three Scriptural Collections And Three Objects To Be Known

The three final reasons for positing three scriptural collections are: The *sets of discourses* are for the purpose of expounding doctrines and their meanings. The *discipline* is posited from the viewpoint of establishing doctrines and their meanings [in practice], and *manifest knowledge* is for the purpose of becoming skilled in discourse relating doctrines and their meanings.

The way in which the sets of discourses expound doctrines and meanings is that they extensively explain doctrines – letters, stems, and words – and meanings – the aggregates, constituents, sources, etc. that are expressed by them. [29] Or, they explain doctrines such as the aggregates, constituents, etc. and meanings – the four thoughts [behind them] *(dgongs pa, abhiprāya)* and the four intentions *(ldem dgongs, abhisandhi)*.[18] Or, they explain the doctrines of the ten virtuous paths [described in the next chapter] bringing about attainment of high status [within cyclic existence] and the meaning of the thirty-seven harmonies with enlightenment *(byang chub kyi phyogs, bodhipakṣa)*[19] – the paths bringing about the attainment of the qualities of definite goodness [liberation from cyclic existence and omniscience]. From that point of view, the sets of discourses train one in words and meanings.

The way in which doctrines and meanings are established through the scriptural collection of the discipline is that the afflictions are subdued through the teaching of the application of pure ethics as well as through teaching meditation on the impure and so forth; thereby, the doctrines and meanings propounded earlier are understood and realized through becoming manifest in the mental continuum. As a result, doctrines and meanings are established through the scriptural collection of the discipline. Through the scriptural collection of manifest knowledge, one becomes skilled in discourse relating doctrines and their meanings.

All the pronouncements of the Conqueror that teach the essentials of method and wisdom in the practice of the three vehicles [of Hearers, Solitary Realizers, and Bodhisattvas] are included in the three scriptural collections by way of these nine reasons.

THREE TRAININGS

When all topics of the three scriptural collections themselves are included [into broad categories], they are included either directly or ancillarily in the practice of the three trainings:

the training in special ethics, the training in special meditative stabilization, and the training in special wisdom. [30]

The ethics set forth by the Buddha are special because they directly and indirectly benefit everyone, both oneself and others. Austerities and ethics such as using the five fires [to bake oneself to death] taught in other systems of doctrine, such as those of the [non-Buddhist] Forders *(mu stegs pa, tīrthika)*, are inferior because they directly or indirectly bring misery to oneself and others.

Similarly, the meditative stabilizations set forth by the Buddha are special because, by serving as antidotes to afflictions and [mis]conceptions, they bring happiness not only in this lifetime but also in other lifetimes, as well as the happiness of liberation. The meditative stabilizations of non-Buddhists are inferior because they are incapable of doing anything other than providing happiness in this lifetime by turning the mind away from distraction outward and have no better effect than causing birth as a god in the Form and Formless Realms. [31] They do not serve as antidotes to afflictions and [mis]conceptions.

The wisdom explained in the Buddha's pronouncements is special because it is able, either directly or indirectly, to clear away all obstructions – the conceptions of the two selves [self of persons and self of phenomena]. The wisdom explained by non-Buddhists is inferior because it is incapable of severing the root of cyclic existence through seeing the mode of subsistence [of phenomena]. For these reasons, the ethics, meditative stabilization, and wisdom set forth by the Buddha are superior to others. Hence, they are called the three *special* trainings *(lhag pa'i bslab pa, adhiśikṣā)*.

4 *Training in Special Ethics*

The first of the three special trainings, that in special ethics, is the basis of all good qualities and is the quintessence of the practices taught by the Buddha. [32] Nāgārjuna's *Friendly Letter (bshes pa'i springs yig, suhṛllekha)* says:[20]

> [The Buddha] said that ethics is the foundation of all good qualities
> Just as the earth is [the basis] of the moving and unmoving.

There are many enumerations of ethics based on the ethics abandoning the ten non-virtues. If these are condensed, they can be included within three types: the ethics of individual liberation *(so thar gyi tshul khrims, pratimokṣaśīla)*, Bodhisattva ethics, and the ethics of Secret Mantra.

Ethics Abandoning the Ten Non-Virtues

The master Vasubandhu's *Treasury of Knowledge* (IV.66) says:[21]

> Collected from those [good and bad activities],[22]
> The major ones are set forth as the ten paths of action,
> Either virtuous or non-virtuous.

The ethics abandoning the ten non-virtues are rules for abandoning these ten:

1 the three physical non-virtues of killing, stealing, and sexual misconduct
2 the four verbal non-virtues of lying, divisive speech, harsh speech, and senseless talk [33]
3 the three mental non-virtues of covetousness, harmful intent, and wrong view.

Through the paths of the three doors [of body, speech, and mind] the ten paths of actions are performed and accumulated.

Killing. Killing has five branches. The *basis* is a sentient being other than oneself. The *thought* is to identify that being without error. The *execution* [of the action] is to kill the being oneself or to cause another to kill him or her using poison, weapons, knowledge-mantra [magic], and so forth. The *affliction* is, in general, desire, hatred, or obscuration, but specifically hatred. The *completion* occurs when the person to be killed dies before one oneself dies.

A path of the action of killing is completed through these five branches. If any of the branches is not present, the deed is a faulty deed but not a complete path of action. This also should be known with respect to the remaining non-virtues.

When killing is divided, there is killing due to desire such as killing out of attachment to meat, killing due to enmity such as in revenge, and killing due to obscuration such as in animal sacrifice. Within killing, to kill such persons as a Foe Destroyer *(dgra bcom pa, arhan),* one's teacher, a parent, a practitioner of virtue, or a renunciate are very great ill-deeds. [34]

Stealing. The *basis* is an article considered to be someone else's possession, an article dedicated to the Three Jewels, etc. The *thought* is a motivation wanting to take [that possession] by deceit, force, or burglary. The *execution* is to do this oneself or cause another to do so. The *affliction* is generally the three poisons but specifically desire. The *completion* is to remove that article from its place, or even though not having removed it, to think that one has acquired it. The three types of stealing are robbery by force, as in the case of forcible robbery of the innocent, robbery by burglary, such as in breaking into a house, and robbery by deceit, such as in using inaccurate scales. Among the types of stealing, stealing the possessions of the Three Jewels is a very great ill-deed.

Sexual Misconduct. The *basis* is an unsuitable partner, such as the spouse of another, a close relative up to seven times removed, or a nun or monk who is keeping vows, or in an unsuitable location, such as with your spouse near an image of the Three Jewels, or in an unsuitable orifice, that is, any orifice other than the vagina, or at an unsuitable time, such as during the observance of precepts for one day, during pregnancy or a menstrual period, or during the day. The *thought* is the motivation of desire to copulate. The *execution* is to undertake that action. The *affliction* is the three poisons but specifically desire. The *completion* is take personal gratification by way of attachment to the experience of pleasurable feeling that arises from the contact of the two organs.

There are three types of sexual misconduct: with someone under the protection of the family, such as one's parent or sibling, with someone protected by a spouse, with someone protected by religion, such as a nun or monk. [35] From among perverse desires, deviant behaviour with someone who is both one's parent and a Foe Destroyer is a very great ill-deed.

Lying. The *basis* is a person other than oneself. The *thought* is the motivation wishing to say, for example, "I saw such and such," when one did not see it, with the intention to mislead someone. The *execution* is the communication of that either physically or verbally. The *affliction* may be any of the three poisons. The *completion* is for another to understand the meaning. The *execution* of this is not necessarily in verbal communication or verbal expression; there are also cases of falsehood through physical gestures.

There are three types of lying. Falsity leading to downfall is, for example, to pretend to have achieved superhuman qualities, that is, high qualities, which one has not achieved. [The other two types are] great falsehood that brings help or harm to oneself or others and a slight lie that does not help or harm. Within the various types of falsehood, deprecating a Buddha and deceiving one's guru, parents, and so forth are very great ill-deeds.

Divisive speech. The *basis* is others who are in a state of harmony. [36] The *thought* is the desire to divide them. The *execution* is to undertake that action. The *affliction* is the three poisons, specifically hatred. The *completion* is the other party's understanding the meaning. Acting with the intention to cause further disagreement between enemies who are seeking reconciliation is also included in this.

There are three types of divisive speech: overt divisiveness as in directly separating friends, indirect divisiveness such as causing division through implication, and covert divisiveness such as causing dissension deceptively. Among the types of divisive speech, causing dissension between teacher and student or within the spiritual community is a very great ill-deed.

Harsh speech. The *basis* is included in the continuum of a sentient being.[23] The *thought* is a motivation wanting to say something unpleasant. The *execution* is to strive to do so. The *completion* is its issuance in communication. The *affliction* is any of the three but specifically hatred.

There are three types of harsh speech: harsh speech to the face, such as saying something bad directly to another, covert harsh words, such as saying a bad word to another in jest, and indirect harsh speech, such as saying something bad to another's friends. [37] Among the types of harsh speech, to speak harshly to one's parents or to a Superior *('phags pa, āryan)* is a very great ill-deed.

Senseless talk. The *basis* is included in the continuum of another. The *thought* is a motivation wanting to speak nonsensically out of non-conscientiousness. The *execution* is to initiate flattery, song, and so forth. The *completion* is issuance in verbal communication. The *affliction* is any of the three poisons but specifically obscuration.

There are three types of senseless speech: wrong senseless

speech, such as the mantra repetitions of [non-Buddhist] Forders, worldly senseless speech, such as telling foolish jokes, and true senseless speech, such as explaining the doctrine to those who are not [suitable] vessels. Among the various kinds of senseless speech, that which distracts those seeking just the doctrine is a great ill-deed. [38]

Covetousness. The *basis* is an internal or external possession of another. The *thought* is a motivation hoping for and wishing for another's prosperity or articles. The *execution* is to think about it again and again. The *affliction* is any of the three poisons but specifically desire. The *completion* is to engage in that action again and again without shame or embarrassment and without resorting to its antidote.

There are three types of covetousness, coveting factors that are one's own, such as attachment to one's lineage, coveting factors owned by another, such as attachment to another's prosperity, and coveting that which is neither of those, such as wishing for treasure under the ground. Among the various types of covetousness, coveting the goods of a renunciate is a great ill-deed.

Harmful intent. The *basis* is included in the continuum of a sentient being. [39] The *thought* is a motivation wishing to harm, such as to kill or strike. The *execution* is an occasion of such an intention. The *affliction* is any of the three afflictions but specifically hatred. The *completion* is to view it as a good quality and not want to apply its antidote. There are three types of harmful intent: harmful intent arising from hatred, such as an intention to kill another in battle, harmful intent arising from jealousy, such as an intention to harm a rival, and harmful intent arising from enmity, such as the wish to harm even though the person has withdrawn any offensiveness. Among the types of harmful intent, the harmful intent motivating a deed of immediate retribution [killing one's father, killing one's mother, killing a Foe Destroyer, causing blood to flow from the body of a Buddha with evil intent, and causing dissension within the spiritual community] is a very great ill-deed.

Wrong view. The *basis* is a virtuous or non-virtuous phenomenon. The *thought* is a motivation to view virtue and ill-deeds as non-existent, to view cause and effect mistakenly, etc. The *execution* is an occasion of thinking such repeatedly. The *affliction* is any of the three, but specifically obscuration. The *completion* is to decide such and not [apply] an antidote. [40]

There are three types of wrong view: wrong view with respect to the effects of actions, such as not accepting that virtues and ill-deeds are the causes of happiness and suffering, wrong view with respect to the truths, such as not accepting that true cessations are achieved even if one practices true paths, and wrong view with respect to the Three Jewels such as deprecating them. Wrong views are the heaviest of mental non-virtues.

The abandonment of these ten non-virtues is called the ethics of abandoning the ten non-virtues.

Vows of Individual Liberation

The ethics of individual liberation are called "individual liberation" *(so so thar pa, prātimokṣa)* because they cause individual persons to be liberated from the suffering of cyclic existence. Their entity is an intention [including the mind and mental factors in association with it] to abandon harming others, as well as its motivational bases [in accordance with] ethical rules that are assumed with the motivation of wishing to leave all of cyclic existence with an attitude of seeking peace for oneself, not merely a [wish for] protection from fear or a wish for goodness [within cyclic existence].

When the ethics of individual liberation are divided from the viewpoint of the base [i.e., the person keeping the vows], there are eight types of vows of individual liberation. Vasubandhu's *Treasury of Knowledge* (IV.14a) says:[24] [41]

> "Individuation liberation" has eight types.
> In terms of substantial entity there are four types.

The eight are:

1 one-day lay devotee *(bsnyen gnas, upavāsa)*

2 layman *(dge bsnyen pha, upāsaka)*
3 laywoman *(dge bsnyen ma, upāsikā)*
4 novice monk *(dge tshul pha, śrāmaṇera)*
5 novice nun *(dge tshul ma, śrāmaṇerikā)*
6 probationary nun *(dge slob ma, śikṣamāṇā)*
7 monk *(dge slong pha, bhikṣu)*
8 nun *(dge slong ma, bhikṣunī)*

One-day lay devotees keep eight vows. Laymen and laywomen keep [up to] five vows each. Novices have thirty-six transgressions; there are also faulty deeds and so forth that are partial concordances and are to be restrained. Probationary nuns must keep twelve vows – six root precepts and six concordant precepts – in addition to the novice vows. The vows of fully ordained monk are the four defeats, thirteen remainders, thirty downfalls [requiring] abandonment, ninety mere infractions, four to be individually confessed, and 112 faults, making 253 rules that must be kept. The vows of fully ordained nuns are the eight defeats, twenty remainders, thirty-three downfalls [requiring] abandonment, 180 mere infractions, twelve to be individually confessed, and 112 faults, making 364 rules that must be kept.[25] [42]

Among the eight types of [vows of] individual liberation, the vows of one-day lay devotees last for one day; if kept for one day, it is sufficient. The vows of the other seven – laymen, laywomen, etc. – last as long as one lives and so must be kept until death.

Furthermore, a recipient of such vows should be free from these obstacles: obstacles to the generation of the vow such as having committed one of the deeds of immediate retribution, obstacles to maintaining [the vow], such as not having legal permission or the permission of one's parents, obstacles to enhancement [of the vow], such as [being so ineffective that one] could not drive away a crow, and obstacles to beauty such as golden hair or a maimed ear. Apart from being devoid of these, there are no distinctions of high or low class and poverty or wealth; if one is able to practice in accordance with one's mental capacity, one is permitted to receive the vows.

The rites by which someone who has not yet obtained vows receives them are of two types, the rites of the past that did not require great hardship [since during the Buddha's time he took people into the spiritual community in a very simple way] and the present rites that must be achieved through great hardship [compared with the uncomplicated procedure when the Buddha accepted people directly]. [43] Also, the way to keep vows already obtained is to keep them through relying on other people, to keep them through pure thought, to keep them through identifying the discordant class, to keep them through thorough training in the precepts, and to keep them through relying on conditions for abiding happily.

The first, keeping them through relying on other people, is to maintain the vows through relying on the advice of a person who has heard much [teaching] and through relying on the model of one with good holy practice. Specifically, having taken full ordination, one should rely on a fully qualified master with whom one resides.

The second, keeping them through pure awareness or thought, is to maintain the vows through not being devoid of *effort,* which is enthusiasm with respect to what is to be adopted and discarded, *conscientiousness,* which is care with respect to what is to be engaged in and turned away from, *mindfulness and introspection,* which examine and analyze one's own continuum, and *embarrassment* in terms of others and *conscience* in terms of oneself. [44]

The third, keeping them through identifying the discordant class, is to maintain the vows through identifying the causes of losing the vows, causes of degeneration of the vows, conditions for their maintenance, and the causes destroying mental clarity – in brief, studying, hearing, and thinking about the texts on discipline.

The fourth, keeping them through thorough training in the precepts is to make effort at the practice of the three basics – purification [of ill-deeds] and renewal [of the precepts], the summer retreat, and the end of the summer retreat.

The fifth, keeping them through relying on conditions for abiding happily means that one must abandon and guard against infractions based on clothing, and similarly those based on food, vessels [such as a begging bowl], and place of residence.

The main causes for the arising of faults are called the four doors leading to infraction: non-knowledge, disrespect, non-conscientiousness, and having many afflictive emotions. One must make effort to protect ethics just as one protects one's eyes, through relying on the aforementioned five means for keeping the precepts as antidotes [to these four]. [45]

Bodhisattva and Secret Mantra Vows

The vows of individual liberation are ethics common to the Small and Great Vehicles, whereas the Bodhisattva vows and the Secret Mantra vows are ethics of the Great Vehicle. Having received the Bodhisattva vows, one must guard against eighteen root infractions and forty-six faulty deeds. Having received the Secret Mantra vows, one must guard against fourteen root infractions, eight gross infractions, and so forth which are common to the five [Buddha] lineages. In addition, there are many enumerations of pledges for the individual lineages.

Since for these two vows, the identifications of the individual divisions which must be kept, the ways of guarding them, and so forth are very vast, I will not discuss them here.

5 *Training in Special Meditative Stabilization*

From among the three special trainings, the second is the training in meditative stabilization. [46] The mind's abiding one-pointedly, without distraction, on any virtuous object is called meditative stabilization *(ting nge 'dzin, samādhi)*. In dependence upon cultivating it, the actual [four] concentrations *(bsam gtan, dhyāna)* and [four] formless meditative absorptions *(gzugs med kyi snyom 'jug, ārūpyasamāpatti)* are attained, and when its cultivation is complete, it finally becomes the perfection of concentration *(bsam gtan gyi pha rol tu phyin pa, dhyānapāramitā)*.

When meditative stabilization is divided in terms of its entity, there are two types – mundane and supramundane. In order to achieve these, one must initially create calm abiding *(zhi gnas, śamatha)* in the mental continuum. Then one must create special insight *(lhag mthong, vipaśyanā)*, and at that point one has created a meditative stabilization that is a union of calm abiding and special insight. The Conqueror Son Shāntideva's *Engaging in the Bodhisattva Deeds (byang chub sems dpa'i spyod pa la 'jug pa, bodhi[sattva]caryāvatāra*, VIII.4) says:[26]

Knowing that special insight endowed with calm abiding

> Thoroughly destroys the afflictions,
> One must initially seek calm abiding.
> It is achieved by those liking non-attachment
> to the world. [47]

The reason why calm abiding must be cultivated first is that all qualities of the three vehicles are effects of stabilizing and analytical meditation, which [respectively] are actual calm abiding and special insight or similitudes of them. When calm abiding has been achieved, all analytical meditations as well as all virtuous activities have great power because the mind is engaged in its own object of observation without being distracted to anything else.

HOW TO ACHIEVE CALM ABIDING

In order to cultivate calm abiding, one must abandon the five faults and utilize the eight antidotes. Maitreya's *Discrimination of the Middle and Extremes (dbus mtha' rnam 'byed, madhyāntavibhaṅga,* IV.3b) says:[27]

> It arises from the cause of utilizing the eight
> Activities [of antidotes] abandoning the five faults.

The five faults are:

1 laziness, which is a lack of enthusiasm for cultivating meditative stabilization
2 forgetfulness, which is the loss of mindfulness of the object of observation itself
3 the mind's falling under the influence of laxity or excitement although the object of observation is not forgotten
4 not making use of the antidotes to laxity and excitement although one has identified that the mind has fallen under their influence
5 even though laxity and excitement are absent, one still does not concentratedly focus on the object but [mistakenly continues to] apply the antidotes to laxity and excitement.

As Maitreya's *Discrimination of the Middle and Extremes* (IV.4) says:[28]

> Laziness, forgetting the advice,
> Laxity and excitement,
> Non-application, and application –
> These are asserted as the five faults. [48]

One should meditate within having abandoned these five faults.

Regarding how to implement the eight antidotes that abandon these, the first of the five faults – laziness – has four antidotes, and the others each have one. The four antidotes to laziness are faith, aspiration, effort, and pliancy. The antidote to the second fault, forgetfulness, is mindfulness. The antidote to the third, laxity and excitement, is introspection. The antidote to the fourth, not applying the antidotes, is an intention of application. The antidote to the fifth, [over-] applying the antidotes, is the equanimity to leave the mind naturally. Maitreya's *Discrimination of the Middle and Extremes* (IV.5-6a) says:[29]

> [The aspiration seeking meditative stabilization which is] the source [of exertion, the effort or exertion] depending on that,
> [The faith seeing the good qualities of meditative stabilization which is] the cause [of aspiration], and [the pliancy which is] the effect [of exertion],
> Not forgetting the object of observation,
> Realizing laxity and excitement,
> The application abandoning them,
> And proceeding naturally when pacified. [49]

One should meditate within utilizing the eight antidotes.

When one meditates in the context of knowing (1) the division of these [preparatory levels of meditative stabilization] into the nine mental abidings, (2) how these are achieved through the six powers, and (3) how these are included within the four mental engagements, one will easily achieve flawless meditative stabilization. The Superior Maitreya's *Ornament for the Great Vehicle Sūtras* (XIV. 11-14) says:[30]

[1] Having directed the mind at the object of observation,
[2] Do not allow its continuum to be distracted.
[3] Having noticed distraction quickly [50] return (the mind) to that [object].
[4] The aware also withdraw the mind inside more and more.
[5] Then, due to seeing the good qualities, tame the mind in meditative stabilization.
[6] Through seeing the faults of distraction pacify dislike for [meditative stabilization].
[7] Desire and so forth as well as discomfort and so forth likewise should be pacified [immediately] upon arising.
[8] Then, those who make effort at restraint make endeavour in the mind.
[9] [Then] natural arising is attained. Aside from familiarizing with that, one desists from activity.

The nine mental abidings are:

1 setting the mind *(sems 'jog pa, cittasthāpana)*
2 continuous setting *(rgyun du 'jog pa, samsthāpana)*
3 re-setting *(slan te 'jog pa, avasthāpana)*
4 close setting *(nye bar 'jog pa, upasthāpana)*
5 disciplining *(dul bar byed pa, damana)*
6 pacifying *(zhi bar byed pa, śamana)*
7 thorough pacifying *(nye bar zhi bar byed pa, vyupaśamana)*
8 making one-pointed *(rtse gcig tu byed pa, ekotīkaraṇa)* [51]
9 setting in equipoise *(mnyam par 'jog pa, samādhāna)*.

The six powers are:

1 the power of hearing *(thos pa, śruta)*
2 the power of thinking *(bsam pa, cintā)*
3 the power of mindfulness *(dran pa, smṛti)*

4 the power of introspection *(shes bzhin, samprajanya)*
5 the power of effort *(brtson 'grus, vīrya)*
6 the power of familiarity *(yong su 'dris pa, paricaya).*

The four mental engagements are:

1 forcible engagement *(sgrim ste 'jug pa, balavāhana)*
2 interrupted engagement *(bar du chad cing 'jug pa, sacchidravāhana)*
3 uninterrupted engagement *(chad pa med par 'jug pa, niśchidravāhana)*
4 effortless engagement *(lhun grub tu 'jug pa, anābhogavāhana).*

The first mental abiding, *setting the mind,* arises when the mind is initially withdrawn inside and placed on the object of observation, not letting it scatter to external objects. This is a result of the first power [the *power of hearing*] – merely listening to instructions on how to set the mind on an object of observation. At that time, the mind, for the most part, cannot stay in place, and thoughts come one after another like a waterfall. One thereby comes to identify thoughts and wonders whether conceptuality is increasing. [However] this is a case of not having previously identified [the array of thoughts], since the mind was not directed inward, whereas now [thoughts] are identified due to having activated mindfulness, like paying attention to travellers on a busy road [whom one ordinarily does not notice]. [52] Hence, there is no fault.

Then, with gradual cultivation, through the second power – *thinking* – one continually thinks about and nurtures the continuum of the mind's placement on the object. When one is able to put together a slight continuity [of placement on the object], the second state of mind, *continuous setting,* arises. At that time, thought sometimes is pacified and sometimes suddenly arises; one has the sense that thought is resting.

In these two states, laxity and excitement are very plentiful, and meditative stabilization is not more than infrequent. One must strive to force the mind to aim at its object;

therefore, this is a time of the first of the four mental engagements, forcible engagement.

Then, gradually through the third power, *the power of mindfulness,* when the mind is distracted from the object to something else, one recognizes it immediately and places it back on the object. At that point, the third mental abiding, *re-setting,* arises.

After that, through initially producing the power of mindfulness, one does not let the mind be distracted from the object of observation, and thus the mind is naturally withdrawn again and again from its extensive range such that it becomes more subtle. [53] With this improved setting of the mind, the fourth mental abiding, *close setting* arises.

Then, by the *power of introspection* – the fourth power – one knows through introspection the faults of conceptuality and of scattering to situations of the secondary afflictions; thus, one does not allow the mind to scatter to those two. Thinking about and taking joy in the good qualities of meditative stabilization, one attains the fifth mental abiding, *disciplining.*

Next, knowing through introspection the disadvantages of distraction, one stops disliking meditative stabilization. At that point, the sixth mental abiding, called *pacifying,* arises.

Then, by the *power of effort* – the fifth power – as soon as a desirous attitude, scattering, laxity, lethargy, or the like is produced in even subtle form, one does not assent to it but abandons it with exertion. At this point, the seventh mental abiding, called *thorough pacifying,* arises.

During the five periods of the third through seventh mental states, even if the stability of meditative stabilization predominates, it is interrupted by laxity and excitement. [54] Hence, these are states of interrupted engagement.

Then, through the power of effort and by using mindfulness, discordant factors such as laxity and excitement are unable to interrupt meditative stabilization, which, therefore, is produced continuously. At this point the eighth mental abiding, called *making one-pointed,* arises. Now, at this time, if one continuously exerts oneself, laxity and excitement are unable to interrupt meditative stabilization, which one is able to sustain for a long period. Hence, this is an occasion of uninterrupted mental engagement.

Then, gradually, due to having meditated [a great deal], through the sixth power of *thorough familiarity,* the exertion of implementing mindfulness and introspection are no longer needed, and the mind engages the object of observation of its own accord. At this point, the ninth mental abiding, *setting in equipoise,* arises. At this time, after the mind has been set once in meditative equipoise through the mindfulness that directs the mind to the object of observation, meditative stabilization is sustained uninterruptedly for a long time through its own force, without needing to rely on mindfulness. Hence, this is an occasion of exertionless mental engagement. For example, if one is thoroughly accustomed to reciting a text or the like, when – upon initially having the motivation to recite it – one begins, [the recitation] proceeds without interruption and without exertion even though, in between, the mind becomes distracted. [55]

This ninth mental abiding in which the mind becomes entirely and effortlessly absorbed in meditative stabilization is a similitude of calm abiding. Through the gradual increase of the slight factor of pliancy that existed earlier, the assumption of bad states preventing the mind from being used in the service of whatever virtue one wishes is pacified, and mental pliancy is produced. Through its power, one separates from the assumption of bad physical states, whereupon a physical pliancy having the nature of a very pleasant physical object of touch is generated. At that time, physically there is a great experience of bliss, and, in dependence on that, a high degree of joy and bliss arises in the mind as well.

When the buoyant mental joy of this time gradually lessens, one achieves an immovable pliancy concordant with meditative stabilization in which the mind abides steadily on its object of observation. [56] Simultaneously, one achieves calm abiding, which is included within the preparations for the first concentration.

THE CONCENTRATIONS AND FORMLESS ABSORPTIONS

Having achieved a fully qualified calm abiding in that way, one gradually cultivates awareness such that from among the three realms and nine levels one separates from attachment to the lower level and thereupon attains an actual [meditative absorption] of the higher level. The three realms are the Desire Realm, Form Realm *(gzugs khams, rūpadhātu)*, and Formless Realm *(gzugs med khams, ārūpyadhātu)*. The nine levels are those of:

1 the Desire Realm *('dod khams, kāmadhātu)*
2 the First Concentration *(bsam gtan dang po, prathamadhyāna)*
3 the Second Concentration *(bsam gtan gnyis pa, dvitīya-dhyāna)*
4 the Third Concentration *(bsam gtan gsum pa, tritīyadhyāna)*
5 the Fourth Concentration *(bsam gtan bzhi pa, caturthadhyāna)*
6 Limitless Space *(rnam mkha' mtha' yas, ākāśānantya)*
7 Limitless Consciousness *(rnam shes mtha' yas, vijñānānantya)*
8 Nothingness *(ci yang med, akiṃcanya)*
9 Peak of Cyclic Existence *(srid rtse, bhavāgra)*.[31]

In dependence upon cultivating such causal meditative absorptions, effects of birth as a god of the Form or Formless Realms occur.

The Seven Mental Contemplations

Concerning how initially to cultivate the concentrations that are causal meditative absorptions, the master Asaṅga's *Compendium of Knowledge (mngon pa kun gtus, abhidharmasamuccaya)* says:[32] [57]

> One enters into absorption in the first concentration through the seven mental contemplations. What are the seven mental contemplations? They are the mental contemplations of individual knowledge of the character, arisen from belief, thorough isolation, withdrawal or joy, analysis, final training, and the fruit of final training.

There are six preparations for the first concentration:

1 mental contemplation of individual knowledge of the character *(mtshan nyid so sor rig pa, lakṣaṇapratisaṃvedī)*
2 mental contemplation arisen from belief *(mos pa las byung pa, adhimokṣika)*
3 mental contemplation of thorough isolation *(rab tu dben pa, prāvivekya)*
4 mental contemplation of withdrawal or joy *(dga' ba sdud pa, ratisaṃgrāhaka)*
5 mental contemplation of analysis *(dpyod pa, mīmāṃsā)*
6 mental contemplation of final training *(sbyor pa'i mtha', prayoganiṣṭha)*.

The first, *mental contemplation of individual knowledge of the character,* is rough investigation *(rtog pa, vitarka)* and fine analysis *(dpyod pa, vicāra)* – by way of a mixture of hearing and thinking – of the lower level, the Desire Realm, as disadvantageous and the upper level, the First Concentration, as advantageous.

The next one, *mental contemplation arisen from belief,* is the generation of just that contemplation into an entity arisen from meditation. The third, *mental contemplation produced from thorough isolation,* is isolation from or abandonment of the three cycles of big manifest afflictions of the Desire Realm. [58] The nine cycles of afflictions of the Desire Realm are:

three cycles of big afflictions
1 big of the big
2 middling of the big
3 small of the big

three cycles of middling afflictions
4 big of the middling
5 middling of the middling
6 small of the middling

three cycles of small afflictions
7 big of the small
8 middling of the small
9 small of the small.[33]

The fourth, *mental contemplation of withdrawal or joy,* is the further abandonment of the three cycles of middling manifest afflictions of the Desire Realm.

The fifth, *mental contemplation of analysis,* is investigation and analysis as to whether one's mind is polluted by the three cycles of afflictions of the Desire Realm. The sixth, *mental contemplation of final training,* is the further abandonment, in dependence upon such analysis, of the three cycles of small manifest afflictions, [the most subtle] of the Desire Realm, through the power of the antidote.

Through these six mental contemplations an actual first concentration, *mental contemplation that is the fruit of final training (sbyor ba'i mtha'i 'bras bu yid byed, prayoganiṣṭhaphalamanaskāra),* is achieved. These mental contemplations, which have the aspect of grossness and peace in that they view the lower level as faulty and gross and the upper level as faultless and peaceful, are clear realizations [i.e., path-consciousnesses] that are common to the mundane and supramundane paths. [59]

The Four Concentrations

An actual first concentration has five branches: the two *antidotal branches* of investigation *(rtog pa, vitarka)* and analysis *(dpyod pa, vicāra),* the two *benefit branches* of joy *(dga' ba, prīti)* and bliss *(bde ba, sukha),* and the *basis branch* of mental onepointedness *(sems rtse gcig pa, cittaikāgratā).*[34] A first concentration that possesses both investigation and analysis is posited as a mere actual first concentration, and one that is without investigation but has analysis is posited as a special actual first concentration.

When one separates from desire for the first concentration through the preparations for the second concentration – such as the mental contemplation of the individual knowledge that the character of the first concentration is faulty and that the second concentration is faultless and advantageous – one attains the second concentration. An actual second concentration has four branches. The *antidotal branch* is internal clarity *(nang rab tu dang ba, adhyātmasamprasāda);* [60] the *benefit branches* are the joy and bliss produced from meditative stabilization, and the *basis branch* is meditative stabilization. Here, internal clarity refers to the three – mindfulness, introspection, and equanimity – of the respective level. Since internal investigation has been completely abandoned, [these three collectively] are called "internal clarity".

When one separates from desire for the second concentration in dependence on the preparations that, by way of the six mental contemplations, analyse the second concentration to be faulty and the third concentration to be advantageous, one attains an actual third concentration. An actual third concentration possesses five branches – the three *antidotal branches* of mindfulness, introspection, and equanimity; the *benefit branch* of bliss, which is such that joy has been abandoned; and the *basis branch* of meditative stabilization.

When one separates from desire for the third concentration in dependence on the preparations that, by way of the six mental contemplations, analyse the third concentration to be faulty and the fourth concentration to be advantageous, one attains an actual fourth concentration. [61] An actual fourth concentration possesses four branches – the two *antidotal branches* of pure mindfulness and pure equanimity; the *benefit branch* of the feeling of equanimity; and the *basis branch* of meditative stabilization. Here mindfulness is said to be "pure" in that it is completely purified of the eight faults of concentration: fire-like investigation and analysis relative to the first concentration, feelings of pleasure and pain accompanying the sense consciousness relative to the second concentration, mental pleasure and displeasure accompanying the mental consciousness relative to the third concentration, and inhalation and exhalation of the breath relative to the fourth concentration.

These branches of the concentrations are eighteen from viewpoint of name and eleven from viewpoint of substantial entity. The master Vasubandhu's *Treasury of Knowledge* (VIII.7-8) says:[35]

The first has five: investigation, analysis,
Joy, bliss, and meditative stabilization,
The second has four branches: [62]
Clarity, joy, and so forth.
The third has five: equanimity,
Mindfulness, introspection, bliss, and abiding.
The last has four: mindfulness, equanimity,
Neither pleasure nor pain, and meditative stabilization.
In substantial entity there are said to be eleven.

With respect to the Concentrations into which one is born as a result of those concentrative absorptions, from having cultivated the small, middling, and great levels of an actual first concentration one is born in the [three] abodes of the First Concentration, the Brahmā Type, and so forth. The same is so for the second and third concentrations, and from having cultivated the small, middling, and great levels of an actual fourth concentration, one is born in the abodes of the Fourth Concentration, the Cloudless and so forth. From completing the small, middling, and great levels of the respective actual concentrations, the fruitional effects and so forth [of that cultivation] are experienced in those abodes. The appearance in form that is produced in the respective abode is a *fruitional effect (rnam smin gyi 'bras bu, vipākaphala);* the mind of absorption is a *causally concordant effect (rgyu mthun gyi 'bras bu, niṣyandaphala);* the appearance of the resources of the area is an *owned effect (bdag po'i 'bras bu, adhipatiphala).*[36] [63]

The Four Formless Absorptions

Limitless Space, Limitless Consciousness, Nothingness, and the Peak of Cyclic Existence are the four possible formless meditative absorptions. The Fourth Concentration having been attained and its not having deteriorated, the sense of touch, sight, and appearance [to the mental consciousness] cease with respect to form, and one meditates that, "All phenomena are limitless like space." The completion of that meditation is the meditative absorption of Limitless Space.

Then, beyond this, one meditates that just as space was limitless, so consciousness is limitless; the completion of this is the meditative absorption of Limitless Consciousness. Then, upon seeing that even both of those involve [coarse discriminative] situations, one meditates thinking that there is no object of apprehension whatsoever. The completion of this is the meditative absorption of Nothingness.

Seeing that even all three of those involve [coarse discriminative] situations, one meditates, thinking, "Coarse discrimination does not exist, and subtle discrimination is not non-existent." [64] The completion of this is the meditative absorption of neither-discrimination-nor-non-discrimination *('du shes med 'du shes med min, naivasaṃjñānāsaṃjñā)* or the meditative absorption of the Peak of Cyclic Existence.

Regarding the effects of those formless absorptions, although the Formless Realm does not have different places distinguished by coarse form, differences do occur by way of superiority and inferiority, length of life, high and low, etc. These effects of pleasure in such high status [within cyclic existence] are more and more sublime in terms of increasingly vast and more stable meditative stabilization, length of lifespan, and so forth.

THE NEED FOR THE CONCENTRATIONS AND ABSORPTIONS

In dependence upon the four actual concentrations, [one can attain] the four immeasurables of love, compassion, joy, and equanimity as well as the five mundane clairvoyances *(mngon shes, abhijñā)* of the divine eye, the divine ear, knowledge of others' minds, memory of former lives, and knowledge of transmigration and rebirth. These are specific qualities [of the meditative absorptions] of the two upper realms [the Form and Formless Realms].

Even those who have entered into the path of the three vehicles must achieve the higher features [of the path] upon having initially produced these meditative stabilizations and qualities. [65] Hence, these serve as the bases of qualities such as clairvoyance. Also, specifically, the absorption of non-discrimination is attained in dependence upon the mind of an actual fourth concentration, and the absorption of cessation, and so forth, are attained in dependence upon the mind of an actual meditative absorption of the Peak of Cyclic Existence.

Therefore, these concentrations and formless meditative absorptions are to be sought and achieved by both non-Buddhists and Buddhists. Since they are also preliminary doctrines for those entering the stages of the teachings of the Conqueror [Buddha], one should, upon coming to know them in this way, train in their implementation.

6 *Training in Special Wisdom*

The third among the three special trainings is that in wisdom. [66] Wisdom is the discrimination of phenomena through investigation and analysis. When it is fully cultivated, it becomes the perfection of wisdom *(shes rab kyi pha rol tu phyin pa, prajñāpāramitā)*. There are three types of wisdom:

1 The wisdom realizing the ultimate realizes the suchness of selflessness either by way of a meaning-generality *(don spyi, arthasāmānya)* [an internal generic image] or directly.
2 The wisdom realizing conventionalities is the wisdom of skill in the five sciences [linguistics, logic and epistemology, arts, medicine, and inner sciences].
3 The wisdom realizing how to bring about the welfare of sentient beings refers to knowing how to achieve the present and future welfare of sentient beings without impropriety.

Among these, one must achieve the most important, the wisdom realizing selflessness. The different schools of Buddhist tenets have a variety of assertions about how to posit the meaning of selflessness, and all of them are in the end just means for realizing the view of the Middle Way Consequence

School *(dbu ma thal 'gyur pa, prāsaṅgika-mādhyamika).* [67] Thus, let us here explain selflessness based primarily on the Middle Way Consequence School.

Chandrakīrti's *Supplement to [Nāgārjuna's] "Treatise on the Middle Way"* (VI.120) says:[37]

> Seeing with their mind that all afflictions and defects
> Arise from the view of the transitory collection [of mind and body as inherently existent I and mine],
> Yogis, upon realizing that the self
> Is the object of this [view], refute self [inherent existence].

The root of all the troubles of cyclic existence and solitary peace is the ignorance conceiving true existence, as well as its predispositions. Apart from the exalted wisdom realizing selflessness – the mode of apprehension of which is explicitly contradictory to that of the ignorance conceiving true existence – there is no means of eradicating [that ignorance]. Therefore, one must make solid effort at extraordinary special insight, the means of realizing the meaning of selflessness.

There are two selflessnesses: of persons and of phenomena. If one ascertains the selflessness of persons, it is easier to ascertain the selflessness of phenomena; therefore, initially one should settle the selflessness of persons. [68]

THE SELFLESSNESS OF PERSONS

To settle the selflessness of persons, it is important to base yourself on the four essentials:

1 the essential of ascertaining the object of negation
2 the essential of ascertaining the entailment [of emptiness]
3 the essential of ascertaining the lack of oneness
4 the essential of ascertaining the lack of difference.

The master Shāntarakṣhita's *Ornament for the Middle Way (dbu ma rgyan, madhyamakālaṃkāra)* says:[38]

> These things propounded by ourselves and others

> Because of lacking in reality [i.e., ultimately]
> A nature of oneness or manyness
> Do not inherently exist, like a reflection.

Ascertaining the Object of Negation

To research the meaning of selflessness, it is very important to identify the object of negation. The master Shāntideva's *Engaging in the Bodhisattva Deeds* (IX.140) says:[39]

> Without contacting the imagined existent
> Its non-existence is not apprehended.

The object of negation is what is conceived by an awareness conceiving true existence.

If one identifies only a coarse object of negation and not the subtle one, one will refute only that coarser one and will be incapable of damaging the conception of true existence because there will still be a remainder of the object of negation. [69] Consequently, one will fall to an extreme of superimposing [true existence onto phenomena]. If, by taking the object of negation too broadly, one holds everything that appears as an object of the six collections of consciousness [eye, ear, nose, tongue, body, and mental consciousness] to be the object of negation, one will fall to an extreme of denying the presentations of conventionalities, whereby the danger of the extreme of annihilation is extremely great.

Through careful analysis of the way in which the I is conceived to be inherently established by the innate [mis]conception of I [as inherently existent, one determines that] the I *appears* to be established as able to stand by itself – to be self-instituting – without depending on the collection of the mental and physical aggregates, which are its basis of designation, or without depending on any of them individually, even though the I appears with those aggregates. That is how [a consciousness] innately [mis]conceiving the I [as inherently existent] operates. Unmistaken identification of this is the first essential of ascertaining the object of negation.

Ascertaining the Entailment Of Emptiness

If the I is inherently established, it must be established as either the same entity as or a different entity from the mental and physical aggregates. [70] The decision that except for these [two possibilities] there is no other way in which it could be established is the second essential – the essential of ascertaining the entailment [that whatever is not established as either the same entity as or a different entity from its basis of designation is necessarily empty of inherent existence].

Ascertaining the Lack of Oneness

If the two – the self and the aggregates – are one entity that is truly or inherently established, they must be an utterly indivisible one. Why? A disjunction of the mode of being and the mode of appearance such that, despite being the same entity, [the phenomena] appear as different [conceptually] isolatable factors or divisions is a mode of falsity of conventionalities. Therefore, if something is truly established, such disjunction of its mode of appearance and its mode of being cannot occur. This is due to the fact that [if there were anything truly or inherently established], the status of that object would have to appear exactly as it is to an awareness to which that truly established object appears.

Hence, if the two – the self and the aggregates – are a truly established unity, there are the faults that:

1 Just as even one person has many [mental and physical] aggregates, so there would be many persons.
2 Or, just as there is no more than one person, so the aggregates also would be one.
3 Just as the [mental and physical] aggregates are produced and disintegrate, the person also would be [inherently] produced and would [inherently] disintegrate.

The realization that the self and the aggregates are not an inherently established unity through such analysis with many reasonings is the third essential of ascertaining the lack of oneness. [71]

Ascertaining the Lack of Inherently Established Difference

If the self and the aggregates are inherently different, it must be a difference that is capable of withstanding reasoned analysis, in which case they must be factually other, unrelated objects that are different in all ways, such as entity, substance, and so forth. Why? Being different from the viewpoint of isolates [that is, being different for thought] but not different from the viewpoint of entity is the status of a falsity. Therefore, such is not feasible in what is inherently established.

Thus, if the self and the mental and physical aggregates are unrelatedly different, when the sickness, aging, and discarding of the aggregates occur, the self would not become sick, aged, and so forth. As a result, there would be the fault that the self would not have the character of the aggregates such as production and disintegration. There would also be faults such as that a separate self would have to be demonstrable upon [mentally] clearing away the five aggregates. Hence, the decision that the self and the mental and physical aggregates lack inherently established difference is the fourth essential of ascertaining the lack of plurality.

Realizing the Selflessness of the Person

A consciousness realizing the non-establishment [of the self and the mental and physical aggregates] either as an inherently established one or as inherently established different [entities] in that way is an awareness realizing the reason – the proof establishing that which is to be proven, an absence of inherent existence. [72]

With regard to how to realize from that [proof] what is being proven, that is, that the self does not inherently exist: for example, when a bull is lost and there are no more than two areas where it could have gone, if someone searches for it in the upper, lower, and middle parts of either field, from merely seeing that it is not in those places the thought is vividly produced that the bull under consideration, the one being sought, is not there. Just so, having previously identified how the object of negation [in this case the inherently existent I] appears to a consciousness conceiving true existence, when – within keeping this [object of negation] deep in the mind – one analyzes with [the reasoning] of the lack of its being one or different, as soon as one has realized [the second reason], the lack of difference, the self that is the object of negation set in the mind disappears. When, at that point, one concludes that such a self does not exist, one has realized the selflessness of persons and found the view of the Middle Way.

THE SELFLESSNESS OF PHENOMENA

The *King of Meditative Stabilizations Sūtra (ting nge 'dzin rgyal po'i mdo, samādhirājasūtra)* says:

> Just as you have known the discrimination of the
> self [as inherently existent to be unfounded]
> Apply this mentally to all [phenomena].
> All phenomena are completely devoid [73]
> Of their own intrinsic entityness, like space.

The selflessness of phenomena is similar to that explained above with respect to persons. If it is illustrated with a pot, for instance, a pot is established in dependence upon the coming together of many dependent-arisings of causes and conditions – its substantial cause, which is the aggregated collection of many minute particles, and its cooperative conditions, such as the activity of the potter's hands. There is no pot that does not depend on any of these but is established as self-arisen and under its own power.

Similarly, there is no phenomenon that is inherently established, that is other than merely established in dependence upon or in reliance upon causes and conditions, its parts, and so forth. While not existing this way, phenomena *appear* to exist this way, and an awareness that conceives phenomena to exist in accordance with how they appear is a consciousness conceiving a self of phenomena.

Having identified the mode of apprehension of such an

awareness, one analyzes by way of the four essentials mentioned above – the essential of ascertaining the object of negation and so forth. At the end of this analysis, the very object of the mode of apprehension of such an awareness destructs into a vacuity, whereupon [the object] appears to the mind as a mere nominally imputed existent, a mere coming together of dependent-arisings. [74] At that point one has realized the selflessness of phenomena.

Through the power of ascertaining in this way that persons and phenomena do not inherently exist, ascertainment of the [validity of] presentations of merely dependently imputed cause and effect, agent and object, is induced even more strongly. Also, in dependence upon ascertaining merely nominally imputed dependent-arisings, ascertainment [of the fact that phenomena] are empty of being established from their own side arises in greater force. When [such mutual reinforcement] occurs, one has realized emptiness as the meaning of dependent-arising and dependent-arising as the meaning of emptiness – the correct view, the Buddha's unsurpassed thought – exactly as it is.

Moreover, there are a very great many such methods for realizing emptiness – not just the reasoning of the lack of being one or different just explained but also the diamond slivers, the reasoning refuting the four extremes, the reasoning refuting the four alternatives, and the reasoning of dependent-arising.[40] [75] When one thus ascertains unerringly the meaning of selflessness – the profound emptiness – by way of many reasonings, [that understanding] should be raised higher and higher through the practice of analytical and stabilizing meditation. This is the way to practice the training in special wisdom.

7 *How to Proceed on the Great and Small Vehicle Paths in Dependence upon the Three Trainings*

In dependence upon practicing these three special trainings, [76] some people progress on the Lesser Vehicle path, achieving the excellent liberation that is the state of a Hearer *(nyan thos, śrāvaka)* or Solitary Realizer *(rang sangs rgyas, pratyekabuddha)* Foe Destroyer *(dgra bcom pa, arhan)*. Some, proceeding on the Great Vehicle Path, achieve the state of a Buddha.

THE LESSER VEHICLE PATHS OF HEARERS

There are five paths of Hearers: those of accumulation, preparation, seeing, meditation, and no more learning. With respect to how these are traversed, Chandrakīrti's *Seventy Stanzas on the Three Refuges (skyabs 'gro bdun cu pa/ gsum la skyabs su 'gro ba bdun cu pa, triśaraṇasaptati)* says:

> Therefore, if one strives at hearing
> For the sake of constant virtue
> Out of [seeking] liberation [from cyclic existence],
> Gradually one becomes a Hearer.

"Cyclic existence" refers to the continuum of [mental and

physical] aggregates appropriated through contamination in which, upon assuming a body due to contaminated actions and afflictive emotions, one powerlessly cycles [in rebirths ranging] from the Peak of Cyclic Existence *(srid rtse, bhavāgra)* to the Most Tortuous Hell *(mnar med, avīci)*. [77] Through realizing just how one is tortured in cyclic existence by the three types of suffering [the sufferings of pain, of change, and of pervasive conditioning], one's mind turns away from that [state of suffering], producing an attitude seeking liberation from cyclic existence. When an authentic awareness seeking liberation develops, one has entered the Hearer *path of accumulation (tshogs lam, saṃbhāramārga)*.

The Hearer path of accumulation has three phases – small, middling, and great. On those occasions, one cultivates meditation on ugliness *(mi sdug pa, aśubhā)*, the meditative stabilization of mindfulness of the inhalation and exhalation of the breath, the mindful establishments *(dran pa nyer gzhag, smṛtyupasthāna)*, the thorough abandonments *(yang dag spong ba, samyakprahāṇa)*, the legs of emanation *(rdzu 'phrul gyi rkang pa, ṛddhipāda)*, and so forth.[41] Through the force of these, erroneous conceptions that what is [actually] suffering is pure, pleasant, permanent, and self, as well as afflictive emotions such as desire and hatred are overwhelmed. As a result, one does not wish for the prosperity of cyclic existence – good resources and the like – and is endowed with the qualities of being inclined toward the direction of purity – liberation – and possession of the five clairvoyances as well as the ability to use emanations and so forth as one wishes. [78]

After that, at the time of the *path of preparation (sbyor lam, prayogamārga)*, not only does one have all the types of qualities of the path of accumulation to a greater extent than before, but also, on the path of preparation, one gradually attains special wisdoms arisen from meditation observing the suchness *(de kho na nyid, tathatā)* of the four noble truths on the occasions of the four levels of that path – heat *(drod, uṣmagata)*, peak *(rtse mo, mūrdhan)*, forbearance *(bzod pa, kṣānti)* and supreme mundane qualities *('jig rten pa'i chos kyi mchog, laukikāgryadharma).* Through that, special clear appearances of the meaning-generalities of the aspects of impermanence, misery, emptiness, selflessness, and so on arise. One also attains the five faculties and the five powers.[42] At that point, one has such inconceivable qualities.

When one passes from the level of supreme mundane qualities on the path of preparation to the *path of seeing (mthong lam, darśanamārga),* through the power of directly seeing the suchness included within the sixteen aspects of the four noble truths,[43] one completely destroys the seeds of all 112 afflictions pertaining to the Three Realms [Desire, Form, and Formless Realms] to be abandoned by the path of seeing. Because one thereby attains the qualities of a Superior *('phags pa, āryan),* one becomes an ultimate spiritual community jewel [from among the three refuges – Buddha, his doctrine, and the spiritual community].

Having attained the path of seeing, one meditates for a long time on suchness, already directly realized, by way of the eightfold path of Superiors in order to destroy the seeds of the *innate* afflictions. [79] The eight branches of the Superior path – the path of definite deliverance – are:

1 correct view *(yang dag pa'i lta ba, samyagdṛṣṭi)*
2 correct realization *(yang dag pa'i rtog pa, samyaksaṃkalpa)*
3 correct speech *(yang dag pa'i ngag, samyagvāk)*
4 correct aims of actions *(yang dag pa'i las kyi mtha', samyakkarmānta)*
5 correct livelihood *(yang dag pa'i 'tsho ba, samyagājīva)*
6 correct exertion *(yang dag pa'i rtsol ba, samyagvyāyāma)*
7 correct mindfulness *(yang dag pa'i dran pa, samyaksmṛti)*
8 correct meditative stabilization *(yang dag pa'i ting nge 'dzin, samyaksamādhi).*

Concerning their entities and functions, *correct view* is, subsequent to meditative equipoise, to ascertain the view in a positive manner, analyzing that in meditative equipoise the reality of the four noble truths was realized in such and such a way. *Correct realization* is to examine through signs and reasonings the profound meaning understood thus and to settle [for oneself] and cause others to understand ways of characterizing how it [the reality of the four truths] and the meaning of sūtra go [together].

Since the nature of reality devoid of [dualistic] elaborations is characterized through words only conventionally, *correct speech* is to cause others to believe the view to be pure by teaching it through explanation, disputation, and composition; it is pure speech free from falsehood and the like. [80] *Correct aims of actions* are pure physical actions such that all types of behavior are without discordance with the doctrine, hence causing others to believe that ethics concordant with the doctrine are pure. *Correct livelihood,* due to its not being mixed with the wrong livelihood of [gaining] sustenance through ill-deeds and its being free from physical hypocrisy, verbal deception, and so forth, causes others to believe that livelihood [concordant with the doctrine] is pure.

Correct exertion, through bringing about repeated meditation on the meaning of the reality already seen, acts as an antidote to the afflictions to be abandoned by the path of meditation. *Correct mindfulness,* through holding the objects of observation and subjective aspects of calm abiding and special insight without forgetfulness, acts as an antidote to the secondary affliction of forgetfulness. *Correct meditative stabilization,* through the achievement of meditative stabilization without the faults of laxity, excitement, and so forth, acts as an antidote to the discordant as well as increases higher and higher the qualities of the path.

When condensed, those eight branches are included in four categories: [81]

1 correct view causes discernment
2 correct realization causes understanding
3 correct speech, aims of actions, and livelihood are branches causing others to believe
4 correct effort, mindfulness, and meditative stabilization are antidotal branches.

The Superior Maitreya's *Differentiation of the Middle and the Extremes* (IV.10) says:[44]

> Causing discernment, causing understanding,
> Three aspects causing others to believe,
> And [three] antidotes to the discordant.
> The branches of the path are those eight.

Through meditating in that way on the meaning of suchness that has already been realized [directly on the path of seeing], one creates an actual antidote to the big afflictions to be abandoned by the path of meditation. At that point, the *path of meditation (sgom lam, bhāvanāmārga)* is attained.

There are two ways of abandoning the afflictions to be abandoned, gradual and simultaneous. Regarding gradual abandonment, one gradually engenders a progression – beginning with the small – of actual antidotes to the eighty-one objects of abandonment by the path of meditation, beginning with the big. [82] The objects of abandonment range from the nine cycles of afflictions to be abandoned by the path of meditation that are included within the Desire Realm and are abandoned by a mundane path of meditation to the nine cycles of afflictions of the Peak of Cyclic Existence to be abandoned by the path of meditation. At the end of gradually creating these eighty-one antidotes, one attains a path of release induced by the vajra-like meditative stabilization of the path of meditation, at which point one attains the Hearer *path of no more learning (mi slob lam, aśaikṣamārga)* or the state of a Hearer Foe Destroyer.

In the case of abandoning the afflictions simultaneously, one abandons the big of the big afflictions of the three realms and nine levels at the same time. Likewise, one abandons the middling of the big afflictions simultaneously, and it is the same through to the small of the small afflictions. Progressing on the path this way, one attains the state of a Hearer Foe Destroyer.[45]

THE LESSER VEHICLE PATHS OF SOLITARY REALIZERS

Chandrakīrti's *Seventy Stanzas on the Three Refuges* says: [83]

> Wanting self-arisen wisdom, those who make effort
> Seeking the enlightenment of a Solitary Realizer,
> Will achieve only the enlightenment
> Of a Solitary Realizer.

Aside from differences in the enlightenment sought and whether or not merit is accumulated for many eons, the five paths and so forth of Solitary Realizers are for the most part similar to those of Hearers.

GREAT VEHICLE PATHS

The Great Vehicle has two internal divisions, a Perfection Vehicle *(pha rol tu phyin pa'i theg pa, pāramitāyāna)* and a Secret Mantra Vajra Vehicle *(gsang sngags rdo rje theg pa, gūhya-mantravajrayāna).* [84] The path of the first, the Perfection Vehicle, also has the five paths, of accumulation and so forth, like the Lesser Vehicle. One attains the Great Vehicle *path of accumulation* when one creates an authentic intention seeking the state of Buddhahood, motivated by love and compassion such that one takes upon oneself the entire burden of achieving help and happiness for all sentient beings tortured by suffering and bereft of happiness. One is then called a Bodhisattva, a Child of the Conqueror [Buddha] *(rgyal ba'i sras, jinaputra),* and a Great Being *(sems dpa' chen po, mahāsattva),* and is worthy of worship by all worldly beings including gods and humans.

As soon as this altruistic intention to become enlightened is produced, Bodhisattvas are endowed with limitless good qualities such as purification of a great many ill-deeds and infractions, swift gathering of great waves of collections [of merit], and the like. At the time of the great path of accumulation, Bodhisattvas achieve clairvoyance in dependence upon an actual concentration, whereby they [can] go to Pure Lands in the ten directions, worshipping and serving many Buddhas. [85] As a result of attaining the meditative stabilization of the stream of doctrine, they hear limitless instructions on the profound [emptiness] and vast [compassionate activities] from those Buddhas and put their meaning into practice.

Then, Bodhisattvas attain a union of calm abiding and special insight observing – by way of a meaning-generality [a general image] – the emptiness that is the lack of true existence of all phenomena; [at that point] they attain the *path of preparation.* The path of preparation has four levels – heat, peak, forbearance, and supreme mundane qualities. On each of those levels the coarse dualistic appearance of true existence becomes more subtle, due to which special clear appearances of the meaning-generality of emptiness gradually develop. The conception of true existence of apprehended objects and apprehending subjects decreases through the force of this.

The signs of achieving peak application are:

1 Through the vast practice of method and wisdom during the day, at night even when dreaming Bodhisattvas view all phenomena as empty of inherent existence, like a dream.
2 They never produce the attitude of the Lesser Vehicle [that is, they never seek only their own liberation].
3 They produce the intention to teach doctrine to sentient beings. [86]
4 They acquire words of truth able to pacify types of harm and injury, such as damage from the four elements [earth, water, fire, and wind], sickness, spirits, and so forth.

Also, Bodhisattvas of sharp faculties, who on the path of preparation achieve the signs of being irreversible from perfect enlightenment, have amazing, inexpressible qualities.

Then, at the uninterrupted path of the Great Vehicle's *path of seeing,* Bodhisattvas directly perceive emptiness and abandon simultaneously the 112 artificial obstructions to liberation pertaining to the Three Realms. Simultaneously, that path also abandons the seeds of the 108 artificial obstructions to omniscience.

When such a path of seeing is attained, Bodhisattvas abandon the sufferings of birth, aging, sickness, and death that are under the control of the other – [contaminated] actions and afflictive emotions. Also, since they attain the meditative stabilization called "proceeding blissfully with all phenomena," no matter what dangerous conditions they encounter – poison, weapons, fire, and so forth – there is only bliss; no suffering whatsoever occurs. [87]

Then, by means of the ten Bodhisattva grounds ranging from that part of the first Bodhisattva ground included within the *path of meditation* through the tenth ground, the qualities of having destroyed the discordant class of objects of abandonment increase, such as the gradual abandonment of the seeds of the sixteen afflictions and the 108 obstructions to omniscience to be abandoned by the path of meditation. The ten grounds are:

1 Very Joyful *(rab tu dga' ba, pramuditā)*
2 Stainless *(dri ma med pa, vimalā)*
3 Luminous *('od byed pa, prabhākarī)*
4 Radiant *('od 'phro ba, arciṣmatī)*
5 Difficult To Overcome *(sbyang dka' ba, sudurjayā)*
6 Manifest *(mngon du gyur pa, abhimukhī)*
7 Gone Afar *(ring du song ba, dūraṃgama)*
8 Immovable *(mi g.yo ba, acalā)*
9 Good Intelligence *(legs pa'i blo gros, sādhumatī)*
10 Clouds of Doctrine *(chos kyi sprin, dharmameghā)*.[46]

On the individual ten grounds Bodhisattvas are endowed with qualities that are inconceivable and inexpressible, special features of thorough purification, and signs for each ground – worshipping and serving many hundreds of thousands of hundreds of billions of Buddhas, apprehending [their] excellent doctrine, and ripening limitless sentient beings through the four means of gathering students *(bsdu ba'i dngos po bzhi, catuḥsaṃgrahasvastu)* [(1) giving material things, (2) speaking pleasantly about how to gain high status within cyclic existence and the definite goodness of liberation and omniscience, (3) causing others to practice what is helpful, and (4) practicing what one teaches others], etc. [88]

Gradually progressing over the ten grounds, Bodhisattvas finally sever the continuum of the subtle obstructions to omniscience through the uninterrupted path at the end of the continuum [of a being who has obstructions yet to be removed] and attain Buddhahood with its limitless qualities.[47]

8 *Brief Discussion of the Secret Mantra Great Vehicle*

Tripiṭakamāla's *Lamp for the Three Modes (tshul gsum gyi sgron ma, nayatrayapradīpa)*[48] says: [89]

> Though the aim is the same, the Mantra Vehicle
> Is superior due to (being for) the non-obscured,
> Having many skillful methods, non-difficulty,
> And being designed for those of sharp faculties.

The Secret Mantra Vajra Vehicle of the Great Vehicle is greatly superior to the Perfection Vehicle. However, the Buddhahoods that are the final objects of attainment, or results, of this vehicle and the Perfection Vehicle do not differ in terms of quality or level. The difference between the two vehicles must be made in terms of the causes that are the means for attaining the effect, the state of Buddhahood.

Concerning that, just as the effect, the Bodies of a Buddha, has two aspects – Truth *(chos sku, dharmakāya)* and Form *(gzugs sku, rūpakāya)* Bodies – so there must be individual uncommon causes of these. The Sūtra and Mantra Vehicles accord [in holding] that the wisdom realizing emptiness conjoined with the altruistic intention to become enlightened is the uncommon cause of the Truth Body and a cooperative condition of the Form Body. [90] However, the Secret Mantra Vajra Vehicle has a vast method [deity yoga], which is an uncommon cause of the Form Body, which the Perfection Vehicle lacks; it merely has the methods of engendering an altruistic intention to become enlightened, the six perfections, and so forth.

Consequently, Buddhahood cannot be attained in one lifetime in dependence upon the Perfection Vehicle but is attained over many lifetimes, whereas in dependence upon the path of the Mantra Vehicle, a person of superior faculties can become fully enlightened in one lifetime or even in several years. Hence, the difference in speed in the Secret Mantra Vehicle is very great.

What is the uncommon cause of a Form Body that is a distinctive feature of the Vajra Vehicle? It is the unsurpassed method of cultivating deity yoga in which one meditates on a body, abode, resources, and activities similar in aspect to those of a Buddha's Form Body in the effect state. The Perfection Vehicle lacks this vast method.[49] [91]

DIVISIONS OF SECRET MANTRA

Within the Secret Mantra Vehicle there are four basic sets of tantras in accordance with the levels of disciples' faculties. The thirteenth chapter of the *Vajrapañjara Tantra (rdo rje gur, vajrapañjara)* says:[50]

> Action Tantras are for the low.
> Yoga without actions is for those above them.
> The supreme Yoga is for supreme beings.
> Highest Yoga is for those above them.

Also, in each of these there are a great many differences such as numerous subdivisions, different entities of their paths, different enumerations, different modes of teaching in the tantra sets, different speeds on the path, and so forth. The details and subtleties of their essential points are suitable to be taught in secret to disciples who have become vessels through having entered a mandala of the Vajra Vehicle and whose minds have been ripened through initiation. However, it is not suitable that they be proclaimed in the marketplace. Thus, because of this inappropriateness, I will not elaborate on the details here.[51] [92]

THE GENERAL STRUCTURE OF THE PRACTICE OF SECRET MANTRA

A person who has experienced the wish to leave cyclic existence as well as the altruistic intention to become enlightened or who, in the absence of such, has previously experienced these to some degree first receives initiation in a mandala of the appropriate tantra-set from a fully qualified lama. Then, the practitioner keeps the pledges and vows in the proper way and, with this as his or her basis, one-pointedly imagines the circle of a deity, this constituting the class of appearances. Through that practice, the Form Body of a Buddha is achieved.

Also, through becoming skilled in the techniques of putting concentrative emphasis on internal winds [or energies] *(rlung, prāṇa),* channels *(rtsa, nāḍī),* essential constituents *(khams, dhātu),* and so forth, the mind enters into the sphere of the Great Seal *(phyag rgya chen po, mahāmudrā)* of clear light devoid of [dualistic] elaborations. Through being absorbed in this yoga, the resultant Wisdom Truth Body of a Buddha is achieved.[52]

9 *The Four Bodies, Qualities, and Activities of Buddhahood*

In dependence upon the paths of sūtra and mantra mentioned above, [93] Bodhisattvas attain the resultant Four Bodies of a Buddha – Nature Body *(ngo bo nyid sku, svabhāvikakāya)*, Wisdom Truth Body *(ye shes chos sku, jñānadharmakāya)*, Enjoyment Body *(longs sku, sambhogakāya)*, and Emanation Body *(sprul sku, nirmāṇakāya)*. The Superior Maitreya's *Ornament for Clear Realization (mngon rtogs rgyan, abhisamayālaṃkāra*, I.17) says:[53]

> The Nature, Complete Enjoyment,
> And likewise Emanation
> And Truth, as well as activities,
> Are expressed as the four aspects [of Buddha Bodies].

NATURE BODY

Through the vajra-like [or diamond-like] meditative stabilization at the end of the continuum of the ten grounds, Bodhisattvas exhaustively abandon the obstructions to omniscience. When the path of release induced by that uninterrupted path is attained, they attain the Nature Body which is the state of having abandoned all adventitious defilements *(glo bur gyi dri ma, āgantukamala)* – the obstructions to liberation and the obstructions to omniscience. This is a factor of purity from adventitious defilements.

Also, the emptiness of true existence of the mind that previously, during the ordinary state, was posited as the naturally abiding lineage *(rang bzhin gnas rigs, prakṛtiṣṭha-gotra)* [providing the capacity to develop into Buddhahood] becomes fully transformed. [94] At that point, it becomes the emptiness of the omniscient mind of a Buddha. It is a factor of natural purity. The Truth Body endowed with these two purities – purity from adventitious defilements and natural purity – is the Nature Truth Body. Although it occurs only when Buddhahood is attained, it is not impermanent – it is not constructed through causes and conditions. It has a nature of permanence, that is, not changing into something of another nature.

WISDOM TRUTH BODY

A Wisdom Truth Body is the exalted omniscient wisdom directly perceiving all modes and varieties of objects of knowledge as if they were in front of oneself. When it is divided in terms of conceptual isolates, there are twenty-one categories of uncontaminated exalted wisdom – ranging from the thirty-seven harmonies with enlightenment through to exalted knowledge of all aspects. These will become clear in the explanation of the mental qualities of a Buddha below. The Nature and Wisdom Truth Bodies are directly perceivable only by Buddhas. [95]

COMPLETE ENJOYMENT BODY

A Complete Enjoyment Body is achieved through training in a pure land on the occasion of the paths of learners. It is the Form Body in which a Bodhisattva initially becomes fully enlightened in a special place [called] a Heavily Adorned

Highest Pure Land *('og min stug pa bkod pa, akaniṣṭhaghanavyūha)*. Having five certainties, it is the basis of emanation of a supreme Emanation Body. Those five certainties are:

1 definite abode: it dwells only in a Heavily Adorned Highest Pure Land.
2 definite body: it is clearly and fully adorned with the thirty-two major marks and eighty minor marks.
3 definite retinue: it is surrounded only by Bodhisattva Superiors; common beings as well as Hearers and Solitary Realizer Superiors are incapable of meeting it.
4 definite doctrine: it teaches just the doctrines of the Great Vehicle, it does not set forth the doctrines of the Low Vehicle.
5 definite time: it dwells without displaying the aspects of birth or death until cyclic existence has been emptied.

A Form Body having all five certainties is an object within the sphere of activity of Great Vehicle Superiors who have directly perceived the truth. Therefore, it is called an Enjoyment Body [enjoyed or used by Great Vehicle Superiors]. [96]

EMANATION BODY

An Emanation Body is a Form Body that can be met even by disciples who are common beings; it does not possess the five certainties. There are three types – supreme Emanation Bodies, artisan Emanation Bodies, and birth Emanation Bodies. A supreme Emanation Body must be identified as one emanated by a Complete Enjoyment Body, adorned with the major and minor marks, that brings about the welfare of disciples through twelve deeds in various world systems, such as Jambudvīpa [this world]. An example is the teacher [of this era] Shākyamuni Buddha.

The twelve deeds, in the case of Shākyamuni, are:

1 descent from the Joyous Pure Land *(dga 'ldan, tuṣita)* [to this world]
2 entry into his mother's womb

3 birth in Lumbinī Garden
4 becoming skilled in the arts and playing the sports of youth
5 taking charge of the kingdom and keeping a harem
6 upon going to the four gates of the city, becoming discouraged with cyclic existence and, due to that attitude, leaving the householder's life [97]
7 practicing austerities for six years at the Nairañjanā River
8 going to the Bodhi Tree and sitting [in meditation under it]
9 overcoming all the hosts of demons
10 becoming fully enlightened on the fifteenth day of the fourth month
11 turning the wheel of doctrine on the fourth day of the sixth month
12 passing from sorrow in the city of Kushinagara.

To the sight of ordinary disciples, some of those twelve deeds are of the Bodhisattva [Shākyamuni before attaining enlightenment], and others are [his] deeds [after becoming a] Buddha. However, all twelve are just displays of such [activities] out of a Buddha's skill in means for taming disciples; all of them – beginning from descent from the Joyous Pure Land – are only deeds of a Buddha [since he actually was enlightened many eons earlier].

An artisan Emanation Body is, for instance, the teacher Shākyamuni's emanation in the form of a lute player in order to subdue the king of the Gandharvas, Sunanda.[54] [98] A birth Emanation Body is, for instance, the devaputra Shvetaketu in the Joyous Pure Land.[55]

From among the Four Bodies, the Nature Body and Wisdom Truth Body cannot be seen by disciples. Both Form Bodies, the Enjoyment Body and Emanation Body, fulfill the welfare of transmigrators on a grand scale through appearing directly to disciples.

Besides the fourfold division of Buddha Bodies described above, these can be treated as three – Truth Body, Enjoyment Body, and Emanation Body – through including the Nature Body and Wisdom Truth Body from among the Four Bodies into one as the Truth Body. These Four Bodies also can be treated as two – Truth Body and Form Body – through including the Enjoyment Body and Emanation Body into one as the Form Body.

There are many approaches for dividing the qualities of such a Buddha, the effect. Let us explain them from the viewpoint of the following four – body, speech, mind, and activities.

Qualities of Body

The physical qualities are the thirty-two major marks and eighty minor marks. The thirty-two marks of a great being are, for instance, the golden wheels on the palms of the hands and soles of the feet glittering very brightly like a bas relief. [99] The eighty minor marks are, for instance, fingernails red like the color of copper and an oily complexion.[56]

Through merely seeing such a beautiful body bedecked with these adornments, special seeds of liberation can be produced. Since the entities of the major and minor marks are not like our contaminated aggregates but are of the essence of omniscient wisdom, each of the major and minor marks of a Buddha, and even each hair on a Buddha's head, directly perceives all objects of knowledge.

Buddhas set sentient beings on salutary paths by way of deeds appropriate for each particular disciple, displaying various physical creations simultaneously in limitless lands of the ten directions like optical illusions. In some lands they display birth; in some, turning the wheel of doctrine; in some, the manner of training in the Bodhisattva deeds; in some, the manner of passing beyond sorrow. [100]

In a single hair-pore of their body Buddhas can display clearly all the bodies and arrays of lands of all Buddhas of the three times [past, present, and future] as well as all practices of the path of those who are still learning. Such are the physical qualities.

Qualities of Speech

The speech of a Buddhas is pleasant because it produces and furthers roots of virtue in the individual continuums of others in accordance with their dispositions and interests. Their speech is soft because it creates happiness of mind in listeners just by hearing it. It is agreeable because it teaches wholesome topics such as the two truths and dependent-arising. Because the elements of the words are well [constructed], it is cogent. These are some of the sixty-four qualities of melodious speech[57] that are fully present in even a portion of a Buddha's speech.

Specifically, when even single word of a One Gone Thus *(de bzhin gshegs pa, tathāgata)* [a Buddha] emerges, the transmigrators – who are gathered there – such as gods, nāgas, humans, and animals – understand it in their own language, and their own particular doubts are removed. Such are the qualities of speech. [101]

Qualities of Mind

With respect to the qualities of exalted wisdom, there are the twenty-one categories of uncontaminated exalted wisdom. Setting aside the categories that are held in common with Hearers and Solitary Realizers, among the unshared qualities of a Buddha are the ten powers:

1. knowledge of sources and non-sources
2. knowledge of actions and their fruitions
3. knowledge of the concentrations, meditative liberations, and so forth
4. knowledge of superior and non-superior faculties
5. knowledge of the varieties of inclinations
6. knowledge of the divisions of the eighteen constituents and so forth
7. knowledge of the paths leading to all forms of cyclic existence and solitary peace
8. knowledge remembering former states [earlier lives]
9. knowledge of death, transmigration, and birth
10. knowledge of contaminations and their extinction.

The four fearlessnesses are the facts, [once Buddhahood has been attained], of there being no one who could properly dispute:

1 the assertion that, in terms of their own welfare, [Buddhas] have attained the marvelous fulfillment of realization directly knowing all phenomena
2 the assertion that, in terms of their own welfare, they have attained the marvelous fulfillment of abandonment, which is extinction of all obstructions
3 the assertion that, in terms of others' welfare, desire and so forth are obstacles to liberation [102]
4 the assertion that, in terms of others' welfare, realization of the status of the four truths is the path of liberation.

The three mindful establishments are the exhaustive abandonments of:

1 attachment to having their retinues listen respectfully when they teach doctrine
2 anger at the disrespectful
3 both attachment and anger at those who have a mixture of respect and disrespect.

The three non-defenses are that one does not – upon fearing that others would know one's faults of the three doors [of body, speech, and mind] – have the thought, "I will conceal those faults."

Since a Buddha is mindful at all times to engage in actions of body and speech for the welfare of others, a Buddha has a nature of not being forgetful. A Buddha has completely destroyed the predispositions of the afflictive obstructions and obstructions to omniscience. A Buddha has great compassion, which is the continual thought during all six periods of day and night to bring about help and happiness for all beings – thinking, "Who is there to be tamed?"

The eighteen unshared qualities of a Buddha are distinctive qualities of a Buddha, not shared with others such as Hearers and Solitary Realizers. These are: [103]

Six included in conduct

1 not being mistaken, such as being fearful and apprehensive about thieves, tigers, and the like when travelling in towns, cities, forests, etc.
2 not having uncontrolled speech, such as letting out loud cries upon losing one's way or bursting out in laughter due to the influence of predispositions
3 not having memory lapses, such as letting an activity slip due to forgetting it, or being late for an activity
4 not having a mind that is not in meditative equipoise on the meaning of emptiness at all times, whether in or out of meditative absorption
5 not having the discrimination of difference that is the conception that cyclic existence is inherently established as unfavorable and that nirvana is inherently established as peaceful
6 not having the indifference of neglecting the welfare of sentient beings upon not individually analyzing the time and so forth for taming them.

Six included in realization

7 the uninterrupted arising of aspiration for love, compassion, bringing about the welfare of sentient beings, and so forth
8 effort that is enthusiasm for going to Buddha Lands surpassing the number of grains of sand on the banks of the Ganges for the sake of even one sentient being [104]
9 constant mindfulness never to forget the styles of mental behavior of all sentient beings as well as the methods for taming them and so forth
10 meditative stabilization set in equipoise on the suchness of phenomena
11 wisdom knowing how to teach appropriately the eighty-four thousand bundles of doctrine as antidotes to the afflictive styles of behaviour of disciples
12 non-deterioration of the release that is a state of having abandoned all obstructions exhaustively.

Three included in activities

13 exalted physical activities such as in emitting light, the four styles of behavior [going, strolling, lying down, and sitting], and so forth

14 exalted verbal activities of teaching what is in accordance with the inclinations of sentient beings

15 exalted mental activities endowed with great love and compassion

Three included in wisdom

16, 17, 18 unimpeded direct knowledge of all objects of knowledge of the past, present, and future. [105]

A Buddha is endowed with limitless unsurpassed qualities, marvelous and fantastic, such as an exalted knowledge of all aspects *(rnam pa thams cad mkhyen pa, sarvākārajñāna)* that directly perceives all phenomena included in the aggregates, constituents, and sources.

A Buddha's quality of mercy is such that there is no situation in which a Buddha does not produce fully developed compassion for sentient beings tortured by suffering. This is due to the power of having brought to completion the great compassion that he cultivated again and again previously, on the path of learning. There are always sentient beings equal to the limits of space tortured by many specific types of suffering, and there is no occasion when a Buddha is unaware of them; hence, a Buddha's great compassion for them also exists constantly without interruption. In dependence upon that compassion, a Buddha uninterruptedly brings about the welfare of transmigrators.

Qualities of Activity

The qualities of activity are twofold, spontaneous and constant. Regarding spontaneity, the sport of a Supramundane Victor's *(bcom ldan 'das, bhagavan)* Form Body – adorned with the major and minor marks – in the four modes of behaviour [going, strolling, lying down, and sitting] and various magical displays is not involved with the conception of exertion. [106]

However, the fortunate, in dependence upon seeing it, engender an altruistic intention to become enlightened, the six perfections, and so forth, whereby they come to attain a state of everlasting bliss. This is the mode of physical spontaneity.

Although a Buddha does not think, "I will teach this," a Buddha teaches limitless doors of doctrine appropriate to the inclinations of disciples. This is the mode of verbal spontaneity.

Aside from the Conquerors' merciful great compassion, a Buddha does not have conceptual motivation, but the rain of excellent doctrine falls, establishing transmigrators in high status [within cyclic existence] and the definite goodness [of liberation and omniscience]. This is the mode of mental spontaneity.

There are no cases in which ordinary worldly beings perform actions without the exertion and striving of body, speech, or mind. However, from the eighth Bodhisattva ground, the coarse exertion motivating the teaching of doctrine and so forth is pacified, whereby others' welfare arises of its own accord. Nevertheless, at that time a Bodhisattva has not abandoned subtle conceptions motivating physical and verbal activity. [107]

The subtle condition opposing spontaneous engagement in the welfare of others is subtle conceptuality motivating involvement in physical and verbal activity. It is called "uncontaminated action" from among the twelve branches [of dependent-arising when these are] classed in terms of the obstructions to omniscience. Therefore, when that is abandoned, the welfare of others arises spontaneously without striving.

Regarding the constancy of a Buddha's exalted activities, earlier, at the time of the path, while gradually traversing the ten Bodhisattva grounds, special qualities included within the two collections [of merit and wisdom] were produced, remained, and increased. Because of the fact that such marvelous causes precede [Buddhahood], a Buddha's activities are constant.

In addition, a Compassionate One [a Buddha] is always considering what assisting conditions there are for destroying the adventitious defilements – the afflictions together with their predispositions – that obstruct the basic constituent of sentient beings, the essence of a One Gone Thus, [the Buddha nature] which in its essence is not polluted by defilement. A Buddha perpetually teaches techniques for destroying these adventitious defilements. Consequently, a Buddha's exalted activities arise spontaneously and constantly. [108]

The chapters above are a brief summary of the essential points of ascertaining the presentation of:

1 the *basis,* the two truths,
2 and thereupon the *path* – the modes of traversing the paths of the Small and Great Vehicles in dependence upon the three trainings, which are the subjects discussed in the three scriptural collections of the word of the Subduer *(thub pa, muni)* [Shākyamuni Buddha], the practice of method and wisdom –
3 as well as the *fruition,* the Four Bodies of a Buddha together with the Buddha activities.

These have not been stated in detail or at length since it would have taken too long.

10 *Tibetan Buddhism*

Let us briefly discuss the systems upholding the good traditions of the doctrine of the Teacher Buddha, the Supramundane Victor, in our country of Tibet. [109] There is no place within the length and breadth of the three provinces of Tibet that was not pervaded by Buddhist doctrines; the teaching spread like the light of the sun.

EARLY DISSEMINATION OF BUDDHISM INTO TIBET

Due to a difference between earlier and later periods, the designations "early dissemination of the teaching" and "later dissemination of the teaching" came to be used. The thirty-second king of Tibet was the religious king song-d̄zen-gam-b̄o *(srong btsan sgam po,* 569-650), who assumed rule at age thirteen. He built the main temples at Hla-s̄a, Tra-druk *(khra 'brug),* and so forth as well as many main temples in three areas called Ta-dul *(mtha' 'dul),* Yang-dul *(yang 'dul),* and Ru-nön *(ru gnon).* He sent his minister Tön-mi-saṃbhoṭa *(thon mi saṃbhoṭa,* fl. 632) to India to study grammar and alphabets. Using Indian scripts as models, he invented a Tibetan script and composed eight treatises on grammar.

The king invited such masters as Kumāra and the Brahmin

Shaṃkara from India and the Nepali master Shīlamañju, who translated many branches of the Buddha's sūtras and tantras, thereby establishing a pathway for the teaching [in Tibet]. [110] Although lecturing on and listening to the [tantric] doctrine were not widespread, the king himself gave instructions primarily concerning the Great Compassionate One *(thugs rje chen po, mahākaruṇika)* – Avalokiteshvara – to many fortunate persons.

Then, the thirty-seventh king, Tri-song-day-d̄zen *(khri srong lde btsan,* 730?-797) came and, seeking to propagate the excellent doctrine, invited the abbot Shāntarakṣhita from Sahor in eastern India and the great master Padmasambhava. The abbot and master as well as those renowned as the 108 great Indian pandits – including the masters Vimalamitra, Shāntigarbha, Dharmakīrti, Buddhagyhya, Kamalashīla, and Vibuddhasiddha – and Tibetan translators such as Vairochana, Nyak *(gnyags)* Jñānakumāram, Ḡa-wa-b̄el-d̄zek *(ska ba dpal brtsegs),* J̄ok-ro-l̄u-gyel-tsen *(cog ro klu'i rgyal mtshan),* and Shang-ye-s̄hay-day *(zhang ye shes sde)* translated various sūtras and tantras spoken by the Buddha concerning discipline, the sets of discourses, and manifest knowledge as well as the more important treatises commenting on their thought. [111] They also established schools of explanation and practice.

The forty-first king, Tri-rel-b̄a-j̄en *(kri ral pa can,* 804–841) appointed seven families for [the support of] each monk and built one thousand temples. Having petitioned the two types of recipients of offering [mantrikas and ordained clergy] to stand on the ends of two pieces of silk tied to his hair, he made offerings to them and revered them. Such were his limitless deeds of reverence for the Conqueror's precious teaching. He invited many leading Indian scholars such as the āchārya Jinamitra, Surendrabodhi, Shīlendrabodhi, and Dānashīla. [Together with] leading Tibetan scholars such as Ratna-rakṣhita and Dharmatāshīla and translators like Jñānasena and Jayarakṣhita, they were instructed by the king to reform the translations made during earlier generations by translating [technical] terminology, which earlier had no equivalents in Tibetan and thus could not be translated, and by improving on passages difficult to understand. In accordance with the King's decree that this be done in harmony with the texts of the small and great vehicles, they reformed the translation of the *Perfection of Wisdom Sūtra in One Hundred Thousand Stanzas,* making it into sixteen volumes, and made definitive translations of most of the scriptures that had been translated earlier, through the formulation of new terminology, etc. [112] This dissemination and propagation of the precious Buddhist teaching to greater and greater levels throughout the snowy land of Tibet is known as the early dissemination of the teaching.

THE LATER DISSEMINATION OF BUDDHISM INTO TIBET

The forty-second king, L̄ang-dar-ma *(glang dar ma,* d.842) suppressed the Buddha's teachings. At that time, three in the lineage of the great abbot Shāntarakṣhita, Mar-shākya *(dmar shākya),* Yo-ge-jung *(g.yo dge 'byung),* and D̄zang-rap-s̄el *(gtsang rab gsal)* escaped to Amdo Province. There, they gave full ordination to the great lama Gong-ba-rap-sel *(bla chen dgongs pa rab gsal),* and from him the number of ordained in Tibet gradually increased.

In addition, the *paṇḍiṭas* Dharmapāla and Sādhupāla from eastern India came to upper N̄gari *(mnga' ris),* and the great Kashmiri *paṇḍiṭa* Shākyashrī came to Tibet, and through their lineages the number of ordained increased greatly. [113] From their time on, many *paṇḍiṭas* and adepts came to Tibet, and many skilled Tibetan translators underwent great hardship to travel to India and Nepal, where at the feet of many scholars and adepts they offered gifts of gold and heard many doctrines of sūtra and mantra [tantra]. They translated these into Tibetan and propagated them in Tibet. The scholars and adepts who followed in their lineages restored the precious teaching of the Subduer [Buddha]. This period when the Buddha's teaching came to shine like the sun throughout the land of Tibet is renowned as the later dissemination of the teaching.[58]

SCHOOLS OF TIBETAN BUDDHISM

A variety of nominally different schools of Buddhist doctrinal systems developed in Tibet. For example, N̄ying-ma-b̄a *(rnying ma ba)* (the Old Translation School) is designated from the viewpoint of time. S̄a-ḡya-b̄a *(sa skya pa)*, D̄ak-lung-b̄a *(stag lung pa)*, Dri-gung-b̄a *('bri gung pa)*, Druk-b̄a *('brug pa)*, and Ge-den-b̄a *(dge ldan pa)* [or Ge-luk-b̄a], for instance, are designated from the viewpoint of the place where they formed. Karma Ḡa-gyu *(karma bka' brgyud)* and Bu-luk-b̄a *(bu lugs pa)*, for instance, are designated from the viewpoint of the name of a master [the former following the Karma-b̄as and the latter following Bu-d̄ön-rin-chen-drup *(bu ston rin chen grub)*]. [114] Ḡa-dam-b̄a *(bka' gdams pa)*, Dzok-chen-b̄a *(rdzogs chen pa)*, Chak-chen-b̄a *(phyag chen pa)*, and Shi-jay-b̄a *(zhi byed pa)*, for instance, are designated from the viewpoint of instructional systems.[59]

All of those schools of doctrine can be included in the two, an Old Translation School *(rnying ma)* and New Translation Schools *(gsar ma)*. How are Old and New differentiated? Great Vehicle doctrines disseminated in Tibet are of two types, sūtra and mantra. Old and New are posited primarily in terms of the dissemination of the Great Vehicle teaching of Secret Mantra rather than in terms of the sūtra class. The translations made during the period of the earlier dissemination, discussed above, up to and including *paṇḍiṭa* Smṛti's arrival in Tibet, are renowned as the early translations of Secret Mantra, and those who bear the system of their explanation and practice are renowned as [followers of] the Old Translation School of N̄ying-ma-b̄a *(rnying ma pa)*.

The translations [of Secret Mantra] made from the time of the translator Rin-chen-sang-b̄o *(rin chen bzang po*, 958–1055) are renowned as the new translations of Secret Mantra. [115] These were begun by the Rin-chen-sang-b̄o in 978 A.D., and subsequently [translators] such as Drok-mi *('brog mi,* 992-1074), D̄a-nak-gö *(rta nag 'gos),* and Mar-b̄a of Hlo-drak *(lho brag mar pa,* 1012-1096) translated many tantric texts into Tibetan and widely propagated the teachings of new Secret Mantra.

The Four Main Orders in Tibet

Among the schools that presently exist in Tibet, there is the Old Translation School of N̄ying-ma-b̄a *(rnying ma)* and the New Translation Schools of Ḡa-gyu-b̄a *(bka' brgyud pa),* S̄a-ḡya-b̄a *(sa skya pa),* and Ge-luk-b̄a *(dge lugs pa).* These four are very widespread and the most predominant.

N̄ying-ma. In 810 A.D. the great master Padmasambhava of Odiyana[60] came to Tibet. At S̄am-yay-chim-pu *(bsam yas mchims phu)* he translated many tantras and means of achievement *(sgrub thabs, sādhana)* such as the eight great sets of achievement. He turned the wheel of doctrine of the Great Secret Vajra Vehicle for a fortunate group including the King (Tri-song-day-d̄zen) and twenty-five ministers. Through the gradual development of its transmission, the Old Translation School of Secret Mantra, N̄ying-ma, was formed.

Ḡa-gyu. In the year 1012 A.D. Mar-d̄ön-chö-ḡyu-lo-drö *(mar ston chos kyi blo gros)* [known also as Mar-b̄a][61] was born. He went to India three times where he met many gurus such as the *paṇḍitas* Nāropa[62] and Maitripāda. [116] He translated and explained authoritative texts, which he transmitted to the venerable Mi-la-re-b̄a[63] *(mi la ras pa,* 1040-1123), the incomparable Dak-b̄o-hla-jay *(dak po lha rje,* 1079-1153) [known also as Gam-b̄o-b̄a *(sgam po pa)*], and so forth. This transmission is known as the Ḡa-gyu School. It has four greater subschools and eight lesser subschools, the four greater being Ḡam-tsang-b̄a *(kam tsang pa),* Dri-kung-b̄a *('bri khung pa),* D̄ak-lung-b̄a *(stag lung pa),* and Druk-b̄a *('brug pa).*

S̄a-ḡya. In 1034 A.D. Ḡön-j̄ok-gyel-b̄o *(dkon cog rgyal po)* of the Kön *('khon)* family was born. From the translator Drok-mi *('brog mi,* 992-1074) he heard [the doctrine of] paths and fruitions *(lam 'bras)* which was transmitted from the glorious Dharmapāla *(chos skyong)*, abbot of Nālanda (whose name upon becoming an adept was Virūpa), and from the great *paṇḍiṭa* Gayadhara. The lineage of transmission from the Five Great Earlier Masters *(sa chen gong ma rnam lnga)* [Sa-chen Ḡun-ga-ñying-b̄o *(sa chen kun dga' snying po,* 1092-1158), S̄ö-nam-d̄zay-mo *(bsod nams rtse mo,* 1142-1182), Drak-b̄a-gyel-tsen *(grags pa rgyal mtshan,* d.1216), S̄a-ḡya *Paṇḍiṭa* Ḡun-ga-gyel-tsen-b̄el-sang-b̄o *(saskya paṇḍiṭa kun dga' rgyal mtshan dpal bzang po,* 1182-1251), and Chö-gyel Pak-b̄a *(chos rgyal 'phags pa,* 1235-1280)] is known as the S̄a-ḡya-b̄a School.

Ge-luk-b̄a. The great scholar of Vikramashīla, Dīpaṃkara-shrījñāna [Atīsha, 982-1054][64] came to Tibet in 1039 where he propagated the profound doctrines of sūtra and tantra widely. The lineage of transmission from Ku-d̄ön *(khu ston),* the translator Ngok L̄o-den-s̄hay-rap *(rngog lo tstsha ba blo lden shes rab,* 1059-1109), and Drom-d̄ön-b̄a *('brom ston pa,* 1005-1064) is known as Ḡa-dam-b̄a *(bka' gdams pa).* The great D̄zong-ka-b̄a *(Tsong kha pa)*[65] was born in 1357 and came to bear the lineage of Ḡa-dam-b̄a. [117] By way of hearing, thinking, and meditating on the full scope of the word of the Supramundane Victor and the valid treatises commenting on their thought that had been translated into Tibetan, he eliminated misconception [in his own mind with respect to their meaning], forming a system of good, unmistaken instruction in the profound meaning of the scriptures. The lineage of transmission through [his students] Gyel-tsap *(rgyal tshab,* 1364-1432), Kay-drup *(mkhas grub,* 1358-1438), and so forth is known as Ge-den-b̄a *(dge ldan pa)* (or Ge-luk-b̄a*(dge lugs pa)*].

Quite a number of people think that the religious systems of Tibet – N̄ying-ma, S̄a-ḡya, Ḡa-gyu, and Ge-luk – differ in the sense that many of their presentations of the bases, paths, and fruitions disagree, like those of non-Buddhist and Buddhist systems. This is not at all the case. To explain the reason clearly, let us take the contemporary example of airplanes. Although they differ in size, shape, and color and differ somewhat in terms of internal machinery due to the skill and experience of the individual designers and craftsmen as well as in how they are equipped, [118] no matter how many types of airplanes there are, they do not differ in the fact that they fly in the sky in dependence upon the force of air and combustion. Just as they must be identified as a single class as all being airplanes, so the differences that exist among the schools of Tibetan Buddhism are merely minor variations in the modes of skillful methods for leading students on the path, having minor differences in terminology, etc., stemming from the respective experiences of the great scholar-adepts who founded the schools.

Aside from these minor differences, these religious systems, in fact, are the same in that their main and final object of achievement is the state of Buddhahood. They are also the same in terms of the stages of practice that serve as the means for achieving Buddhahood in that they do not differ with respect to practicing a union of sūtra and mantra, the inseparability of the three special trainings explained above and a view that does not pass beyond the four seals that testify to a doctrinal system's being Buddhist: [119]

1 All products are impermanent.
2 All contaminated things are miserable.
3 All phenomena are empty and selfless.
4 Nirvana is peace.

Therefore, in the end, they all come down to the same thing.

Some people say that the religion of Tibet is "lamaism", as if it were a religion not taught by the Buddha, but this is not so. The original author of the sūtras and tantras that are the root souce of all schools of Tibetan Buddhism is the teacher Shākyamuni Buddha. Then, in the middle, the great Indian *paṇḍitas*, using reasoning purified by the three analyses,[66] explained and delineated the meaning of the thought of the sūtras and tantras. Also, the great [Indian] yogis who had attained adepthood [set forth] profound instructions [as a result] of authoritative realizations gained upon implementing [those doctrines] in practice. Finally, the Bodhisattva kings and ministers of the snowy land of Tibet and the early kind translators underwent hardships without concern for life or limb – not to mention wealth and resources – [120] and with great effort, like a river with many ships flowing to India and Nepal, heard instructions from indisputably famous scholars and adepts – delighting them with the three delights [making offerings, venerating with body and speech, and achieving what they taught]. It is these doctrines that were translated into Tibetan.

Tibetan lamas took these as the basis and root and thereupon listened to them, thought about them, and meditated on them; among the main points they did not fabricate a single doctrine that does not accord with those [Indian traditions]. For example, any Tibetan Buddhist who has even the slightest need to remove a qualm about a point of doctrine or who needs a source will do so on the basis of sources in the statements of the Buddha or an Indian scholar-adept.[67]

Glossary

English	*Tibetan*	*Sanskrit*
action	las	karma
Action Tantra	bya rgyud	kriyātantra
afflictive emotion	nyon mongs	kleśa
afflictive obstruction	nyon sgribs	kleśāvaraṇa
aggregate	phung po	skandha
altruistic intention to become enlightened	byang chub kyi sems	bodhicitta
analysis	dpyod pa	vicāra
antidote	gnyen po	pratipakṣa
application	'du byed pa	abhisaṃskāra
aspiration	'dun pa	chanda
bliss	bde pa	sukha
Bodhisattva	byang chub sems dpa'	bodhisattva
calm abiding	zhi gnas	śamatha
channel center	'khor lo	cakra
clairvoyance	mngon shes	abhijñā
compassion	snying rje	karuṇā
compositional factor	'du byed	saṃskāra

concentration	bsam gtan	dhyāna
conscience	ngo tsha shes pa	hrī
conscientiousness	bag yod	apramāda
consciousness	rnam par shes pa	vijñāna
Consequence School	thal 'gyur ba	prāsaṅgika
constituent	khams	dhātu
conventional truth	kun rdzob bden pa	saṃvṛtisatya
covetousness	brnab sems	abhidhyā
cyclic existence	'khor ba	saṃsāra
defeat	pham pa	pārājika
definite goodness	nges legs	niḥśreyasa
deity yoga	lha'i rnal 'byor	devatāyoga
dependent arising	rten 'byung	pratītyasamutpāda
Desire Realm	'dod khams	kāmadhātu
discipline	'dul ba	vinaya
discrimination	'du shes	samjñā
divisive speech	phra mar smra ba	paiśunya
doubt	the tshom	vicikitsā
downfall (requiring) abandonment	spang ltung	naiḥsargikapatti
effort	brtson 'grus	vīrya
Emanation Body	sprul sku	nirmānakāya
embarrassment	khrel yod pa	apatrāpya
emptiness	stong pa nyid	śūnyatā
Enjoyment Body	longs sku	saṃbhogakāya
enlightenment	byang chub	bodhi
entailment	khyab pa	vyāpti
ethics	tshul khrims	śīla
excitement	rgod pa	auddhatya
extreme behavior	mtha' gnyis la sbyor ba	
faith	dad pa	śraddhā
fault	nyes ba/nyes byas	doṣa/duṣkṛta
feeling	tshor ba	vedanā
Foe Destroyer	dgra bcom pa	arhan
forbearance	bzod pa	kṣānti
forgetting the advice	gdams ngag brjed pa	avavādasammoṣa
forgetfulness	brjed nges pa	tīrthika

Form Body	gzugs sku	rūpakāya
Form Realm	gzugs khams	rūpadhātu
Formless Realm	gzugs med khams	arūpyadhātu
formless absorption	gzugs med kyi snyoms 'jug	arūpyasamāpatti
functioning thing	dngos po	bhāva
general characteristic	spyi mtshan	sāmānyalakṣaṇa
Great Vehicle	theg pa chen po	mahāyāna
ground	sa	bhūmi
harmful intent	gnod sems	vyāpāda
harmony with enlightenment	byang phyogs	bodhipakṣa
harsh speech	tshig rtsub smra ba	pāruṣya
Hearer	nyan thos	śrāvaka
heat	drod	uṣmagata
high status	mngon mtho	abhyudaya
Highest Yoga Tantra	rnal 'byor bla med rgyud	anuttarayogatantra
holding one's own view to be supreme	rang gi lta ba mchog tu 'dzin pa	svadṛṣṭi-parāmarśa
impermanent	mi rtag pa	anitya
individual liberation	so so thar pa	prātimokṣa
inherently established	rang bzhin gyis sgrub pa	svabhāvasiddha
internal clarity	nang rab tu dang ba	adhyātmasam-prasāda
introspection	shes bzhin	samprajanya
investigation	rtog pa	vitarka
isolate	ldog pa	vyatireka
joy	dga' ba	prīti
Joyous Pure Land	dga' ldan	tuṣita
killing	srog gcod	prāṇātighāta
laxity	bying ba	laya
laziness	le lo	kausīdya

Lesser Vehicle	theg dman	hīnayāna
liberation	thar pa	mokṣa
lying	rdzun du smra ba	mṛṣāvāda
manifest knowledge	chos mngon pa	abhidharma
marks of a great being	skyes bu chen po'i mtshan nyid	mahāpuruṣa-lakṣanāni
meaning-generality	don spyi	arthasāmānya
meditative equipoise	mnyam bzhag	samāhita
meditative stabilization	ting nge 'dzin	samādhi
method	thabs	upāya
mental engagement	yid la byed pa	manaskāra
mental factor	sems byung	caitta
mere infraction	ltung byed 'ba' zhig	śuddhaprāyaś-cittika
Middle Way School	dbu ma pa	mādhyamika
mind	sems	citta
mindfulness	dran pa	smṛti
minor mark	dpe byed bzang po	anuvyañjana
Nature Body	ngo bo nyid sku	svabhāvikakāya
non-application	'du mi byed pa	anabhisaṃskāra
non-functioning thing	dngos med	abhāva
not unable	mi lcog med	anāgamya
object of knowledge	shes bya	jñeya
object of negation	dgag bya	pratiṣedhya
obstruction to omniscience	shes sgrib	jñeyāvaraṇa
One Gone Thus	de bzhin gshegs pa	tathāgata
path	lam	mārga
path of accumulation	tshogs lam	saṃbhāramārga
path of meditation	sgom lam	bhāvanāmārga
path of no more learning	mi slob lam	aśaikṣamārga
path of preparation	sbyor lam	prayogamārga
path of seeing	mthong lam	darśanamārga
peak	rtse mo	mūrdhan
Perfection Vehicle	phar phyin theg pa	pāramitāyāna

Performance Tantra	spyod rgyud	caryātantra
pliancy	shin sbyang	prasrabdhi
predisposition	bag chags	vāsanā
pronouncement	gsung rab	pravacana
remainder	lhag ma	avaśeṣa
rules	khrims	nigraha
scriptural collection	sde snod	piṭaka
Secret Mantra Vehicle	gsang sngags theg pa	guhyamantrayāna
selflessness of persons	gang zag gi bdag med	pudgalanairātmya
selflessness of phenomena	chos kyi bdag med	dharmanairātmya
sense power	dbang po	indriya
senseless talk	ngag 'khyal	pralapa
sentience	yid	manas
sentient being	sems can	sattva
sets of discourses	mdo sde	sūtrānta
sexual misconduct	'dod pas log par g.gyem pa	kāmamithyācāra
Solitary Realizer	rang sangs rgyas	pratyekabuddha
sources	skye mched	āyatana
special ethics	lhag pa'i mtshul khrims	adhiśīla
special insight	lhag mthong	vipaśyanā
special meditative stabilization	lhag pa'i ting nge 'dzin	adhisamādhi
special wisdom	lhag pa'i shes rab	adhiprajñā
specific characteristic	rang gi mtshan nyid	svalakṣaṇa
stealing	ma byin len	adattādāna
Subduer	thub pa	muni
suchness	de kho na nyid	tathatā
Superior	'phags pa	āryan
Supramundane Victor	bcom ldan 'das	bhagavan
supreme mundane quality	'jig rten pa'i chos kyi mchog	laukikāgraya-dharma

to be individually confessed	sor bshags	pratideśanīya
training	bslab pa	śikṣā
true cessation	'gog pa'i bden pa	nirodhasatya
true origin	kun 'byung bden pa	samudayasatya
true path	lam gyi bden pa	mārgasatya
true suffering	sdug bsngal bden pa	duḥkhasatya
truth	bden pa	satya
Truth Body	chos sku	dharmakāya
ultimate truth	don dam bden pa	paramārthasatya
uninterrupted path	bar cad med lam	ānantaryamārga
vajra-like meditative stabilization	rdo rje lta bu ting nge 'dzin	vajropamasamādhi
vow	sdom pa	saṃvara
wisdom	shes rab	prajñā
Wisdom Truth Body	ye shes chos sku	jñānadharmakāya
wrong view	log par lta ba	mithyādṛṣṭi
Yoga Tantra	rnal 'byor rgyud	yogatantra

Bibliography of Works Cited

The bibliography provides references to those Indian texts cited by the Dalai Lama. Sūtras and tantras are listed alphabetically by English title. Indian treatises are listed alphabetically by author. For references to works consulted by the translators and citations of relevant works in English and French, please consult the notes. "P", standing for "Peking edition", refers to the *Tibetan Tripiṭaka* (Tokyo-Kyoto: Tibetan Tripitaka Research Foundaton, 1956).

SUTRAS AND TANTRAS

Heart of the Perfection of Wisdom Sūtra
bhagavatīprajñāpāramitāhṛdayasūtra
bcom ldan 'das ma shes rab kyi pha rol tu phyin pa'i snying po'i mdo
P160, Vol. 6
Sanskrit text and English translation available in Edward Conze, *Buddhist Wisdom Books* (New York: Harper Torchbooks, 1972)

King of Meditative Stabilizations Sūtra
samādhirājasūtra
ting nge 'dzin rgyal po'i mdo
P795, Vol. 31-32
Partial translation by K. Regamey, *Three Chapters from the Samādhirājasūtra* (Warsaw: Warsaw Society of Sciences and Letters, 1938)

Meeting of Father and Son Sūtra
pitāputrasamāgamasūtra
yab dang sras mjal ba'i mdo
P760.16, Vol. 23

Vajrapañjara Tantra
ḍākiṇīvajrapañjaramahātantrarājakalpa
mkha' 'gro ma rdo rje gur zhes bya ba'i rgyud kyi rgyal po chen po'i brtag pa
P11, Vol. 6

SANSKRIT TREATISES

Asaṅga (thogs med)
Compendium of Knowledge
abhidharmasamuccaya
mngon pa kun btus
P5550, Vol 112
fragments and reconstructed Sanskrit text: Pralhad Pradhan, ed., *Abhidharma Samuccaya,* (Santineketan: Visva-Bharati, 1950)
French translation: W. Rahula, *Le Compendium de la Super-Doctrine Philosophie* (Paris: École Française d'Extrême Orient, 1971)

Chandrakīrti (zla ba grags pa)
Supplement to [*Nāgārjuna's*] *"Treatise on the Middle Way"*
madhyamakāvatāra
dbu ma la 'jug pa
P5261, Vol. 98; P5262, Vol. 98; also Louis de la Vallée Poussin, ed., *Madhyamakāvatāra par Candrakīrti.* Biblio-

Buddhica IX (Osnabrück: Biblio Verlag, 1970)
French translation by Louis de la Vallée Poussin up to VI.165 in *Muséon* 8 (1907), pp.249-317; *Muséon* 11 (1910), pp.271-358; and *Muséon* 12 (1911), pp.235-328.
English translation of the sixth chapter by Stephen Batchelor in Geshe Rapten's *Echoes of Voidness* (London: Wisdom, 1983), pp.47-92.

Seventy Stanzas on the Three Refuges
triśaraṇasaptati
gsum la skyabs su 'gro ba bdun cu pa
P5366, Vol. 103

Maitreya (byams pa)
Discrimination of the Middle and Extremes
madhyāntavibhaṅga
dbus dang mtha' rnam par 'byed pa
P5522, Vol. 108
Sanskrit text: Ramchandra Pandeya, ed., *Madhyānta-Vibhāga-Śāstra* (Delhi: Motilal Banarsidass, 1971)
Partial English translation: T. Stcherbatsky, *Madhyānta-Vibhaṅga* (Calcutta: Indian Studies Past and Present, 1971)

Ornament for Clear Realization
abhisamayālaṃkāra
mngon par rtogs pa'i rgyan
P5184, Vol. 88
English translation: Edward Conze, *Abhisamayā-laṃkāra*, Serie Orientale Roma (Rome: Is.M.E.O., 1954)

Ornament for the Mahāyāna Sūtras
mahāyānasūtrālaṃkāra
theg pa chen po'i mdo sde rgyan gyi tshig le'ur byas pa
P5521, Vol. 108
Sanskrit text: S. Bagchi, ed., *Mahāyāna-Sūtrālaṃkāra of Asaṅga,* Buddhist Sanskrit Texts, No. 13, (Darbhanga: Mithila Institute, 1970)

Matṛcheta/Shūra (dpa 'bo)/Ashvaghoṣha (rta dbyangs)
Garland of Birth Stories
jātakamālā
skyes pa'i rab kyi rgyud
P5650, Vol. 128
English translation: J.S. Speyer, trans., *The Jātakamālā* (Delhi: Motilal Banarsidass, 1971).

Nāgārjuna (klu sgrub)
Friendly Letter
suhṛllekha
bshes pa'i springs yig
P5682, Vol. 129
English translations: Lozang Jamspal, et. al., trans., *Nāgārjuna's Letter to King Gautamīputra* Delhi: Motilal Banarsidass, 1978); Geshe L. Tharchin and A.B. Engle, *Nāgārjuna's Letter* (Dharamsala, India: Library of Tibetan Works and Archives, 1979); and Leslie Kawamura, trans., *Golden Zephyr* (Emeryville, California: Dharma Publishing, 1975)

Fundamental Treatise on the Middle Way Called "Wisdom"
prajñānāmamūlamadhyamakakārikā
dbu ma rtsa ba'i tshig le'ur byas pa shes rab bya ba
P5224, Vol 95
Sanskrit text: Louis de la Vallée Poussin, ed., *Mūlamadhyamakakārikās (Mādhyamikasūtras) de Nāgārjuna avec la Prasannapadā Commentaire de Candrakīrti,* Bibliotheca Buddhica IV (Osnabrück: Biblio Verlag, 1970)
English Translations: F.J. Streng, *Emptiness* (Nashville and New York: Abingdon, 1967); K. Inada, *Nāgārjuna, A Translation of his Mūlamadhyamakakārikā with an Introductory Essay* (Tokyo: The Hokuseido Press, 1970); etc.

Shāntarakṣita (zhi ba 'tsho)
Ornament for the Middle Way
madhyamakālaṃkāra
dbu ma'i rgyan gyi tshig le'ur byas pa
P5284 Vol. 101

Shāntideva (zhi ba lha)
Engaging in the Bodhisattva Deeds
bodhi[sattva]caryāvatāra
byang chub sems dpa'i spyod pa la 'jug pa
P5272, Vol. 99

Sanskrit text: Vidhushekara Bhattacharya, *Bodhicaryāvatāra,* Bibliotheca Indica, Vol. 280 (Calcutta: The Asiatic Society, 1960)
English translation: Stephen Batchelor, *A Guide to the Bodhisattva's Way of Life* (Dharamsala: Library of Tibetan Works and Archives, 1979)

Tripiṭakamāla
Lamp for the Three Modes
nayatrayapradīpa
tshul gsum gyi sgron ma
P4530, Vol. 81

Vasubandhu (dbyig gnyen)
Treasury of Knowledge
abhidharmakośakārikā
chos mngon pa'i mdzod kyi tshig le'ur byas pa
P5590, Vol. 115
Sanskrit text: P. Pradhan, ed., *Abhidharmakośabhāṣyam of Vasubandhu* (Patna: Jayaswal Research Institute, 1975)
French translation: Louis de la Vallée Poussin, *L'Abhidharmakośa de Vasubandhu,* 6 vols. (Bruxelles: Institut Belge des Hautes Études Chinoises, 1971)

Notes

1 Among the many prophecies concerning the duration of the Buddhist doctrine after the death of the Buddha, the *Commentary on the One Hundred Thousand, Twenty-Five Thousand, and Eight Thousand Stanza Perfection of Wisdom Sūtras (shes rab kyi pha rol tu phyin pa 'bum pa dang nyi khri lnga stong pa dang khri brgyad stong pa'i rgya cher bshad pa, śatasāhasrikāpañcaviṃśatisāhasrikāṣṭādaśa-sāhasrikāprajñā-pāramitābṛhaṭṭīkā)* predicts that the teaching will last for five millenia, divided into ten periods of five centuries. According to one system of Tibetan reckoning, we are currently in the sixth of the ten periods, called the Phase of Ethics *(tshul khrims kyi le'u)* because during this period there will appear many Superiors *('phags pa, āryan)* endowed with ethics. For a description of the ten periods as well as a discussion of other prophecies concerning the duration of the doctrine, see E. Obermiller, trans., *History of Buddhism by Bu-ston,* Vol. II. (Heidelberg: Heft, 1932), pp. 102-108. Obermiller identifies the source as MDO.XIV 232b.1-7 in the Narthang edition, which is P5206, Vol. 93 (Toh. 3808); the Peking index does not list an author, but the Dharma Press edition lists Daṃṣhṭrasena.

2 According to several Mahāyāna sūtras, Shākyamuni is considered to be the fourth of one thousand Buddhas to appear during the current era. See Obermiller, pp.90–100.

3 P5650, Vol. 128, 51.5.7. For another translation see J.S. Speyer, trans., *The Jātakamālā* (Delhi: Motilal Banarsidass, 1971), p.272. Matṛcheta, Arya-Śūra, and Ashvaghoṣha appear to be names of the same person.

4 This story, as found in *Tāranātha's History of Buddhism in India,* translated by Chimpa and Chattopadhyaya, (Simla: Indian Institute of Advanced Study, 1970), pp. 199-200, reads:

> In the east, (Fol 75A) in Varendra, there lived a *paṇḍita* who attained the vision of Avalokiteśvara. He entered into a debate with a *tīrthika* Lokāyata teacher. He defeated his [*tīrthika's*] views no doubt; yet [the *tīrthika* claimed] that arguments depended on intellect and hence one with keener intellect gained victory. [So he said] 'There is no direct evidence for anterior and posterior existence. So I do not admit this.'
>
> Being thus told, he kept the king and others as witnesses and said, 'I am going to be reborn. Put a mark on my forehead.'
>
> He placed on his forehead a mark of vermilion cut deep into the flesh. Putting a pearl into his mouth, he [the *paṇḍita*] died on the spot.
>
> His corpse was kept in a covered copper-vessel and it was sealed by the king.
>
> According to his promise to be reborn as the son of a *kṣatriya paṇḍita* called Viśeṣaka, a son with auspicious marks was born to the latter. His forehead was found to have the mark of vermilion and within his mouth was found the pearl. On being examined by the king and others, the dead body was found to have no mark of vermilion on the forehead and the place where the pearl was kept was found empty. It is said that the same *tīrthika* then believed in the past and future existence.

5 Cited in Chandrakīrti's *Supplement to [Nāgārjuna's] "Treatise on the Middle Way" (dbu ma la 'jug pa, madhyamakāvatāra)* in commenting on VI.80. See *Madhayamakāvatāra par Candrakīrti,* publiée par Louis de la Vallée Poussin, Bibliotheca Buddhica IX (Osnabrück: Biblio Verlag, 1970), p.175.

6 The Sanskrit is:

dve satye samupāśritya buddhānāṃ dharmadeśanā

See *Mūlamadhyamakakārikās (Mādhyamikasūtras) de Nāgārjuna avec la Prasannapadā Commentaire de Candrakīrti,* publiée par Louis de la Vallée Poussin, Bibliotheca Buddhica IV (Osnabrück: Biblio Verlag, 1970), p. 492.

7 At the direction of the Dalai Lama, four faults (rather than three, as appear in the text) are listed for this position also. See Nga-w̄ang-b̄el-den *(ngag dbang dpal ldan,* 1797-?), *Annotations for (Jam-ȳang-shay-b̄a's) "Great Exposition of Tenets", Freeing the Knots of the Difficult Points, Precious Jewel of Clear Thought (grub mtha' chen mo'i mchan 'grel dka' gnad mdud grol blo gsal gces nor),* (Sarnath: Pleasure of Elegant Sayings Press, 1964), 155.4.

8 See la Vallée Poussin, ed., *Madhyamakāvatāra par Candrakīrti,* pp 301-303.

9 Bracketed material is from D̄zong-ka-b̄a *(tsong kha pa), Illumination of the Thought, Extensive Explanation of* [*Chandrakīrti's*] *"Supplement to* [*Nāgārjuna's*] *'Treatise on the Middle Way'" (dbu ma la 'jug pa'i rgya cher bshad pa dgongs pa rab gsal),* (Dharamsala: Shes rig par khang edition, n.d.), 228.19.

10 Ibid., 228.19.

11 D̄zong-ka-b̄a's *Illumination of the Thought* (229.3) glosses *bzhed pa* as *bshad pa*.

12 *See* Nga-w̄ang-b̄el-den *(ngag dbang dpal ldan,* 1797-?), *Explanation of the Conventional and the Ultimate in the Four Systems of Tenets (grub mtha' bzhi'i lugs kyi kun rdzob dang don dam pa'i don rnam par bshad pa legs bshad dpyid kyi dpal mo'i glu dbyangs),* (New Delhi: Guru Deva, 1972), 185.3. See also his *Annotations for (Jam-ȳang-shay-b̄a's) "Great Exposition of Tenets", Freeing the Knots of the Difficult*

Points, Precious Jewel of Clear Thought, dbu 187.4.

13 The Sanskrit is:

rāśyāyadvāragotrārthāḥ skandhāyatanadhātavaḥ

See P. Pradhan, ed., *Abhidharmakośabhāṣyam of Vasubandhu* (Patna: Jayaswal Research Institute, 1975), p.13. For a more detailed discussion of the aggregates, sources, and constituents, see the first chapter of Vasubandhu's *Treasury of Knowledge (abhidharmakośa)* and Asaṅga's *Compendium of Knowledge (abhidharmasamuccaya),* both of which have been translated into French. See Louis de la Vallée Poussin, trans., *L'Abhidharmakośa de Vasubandhu,* Tome I (Bruxelles: Institut Belge des Hautes Études Chinoises, 1971) and Walpola Rahula, trans., *Le Compendium de la Super-Doctrine (Philosophie) (Abhidharmasamuccaya) d'Asanga,* (Paris: École Française d'Extrême-Orient, 1980).

14 "Discrimination of the small" refers to discrimination in the continuum of an ordinary being in the Desire Realm who has not attained an actual concentration and discriminations observing attributes of the Desire Realm. "Discrimination of the vast" refers to discriminations observing the Form Realm and discriminations in the continuums of beings in the Form Realm. "Discrimination of the limitless" refers to discriminations observing limitless space or limitless consciousness. See Jeffrey Hopkins, *Meditation on Emptiness* (London: Wisdom Publications, 1983), p.243.

15 As listed in J̄ang-ḡya Rol-b̄ay-dor-jay *(lcang skya rol pa'i rdo rje,* 1717-1786), *The Presentation of Tenets (grub mtha'i rnam bzhag)* (Sarnath: Pleasure of Elegant Sayings Press, 1970), p. 90, these are:

1 acquisition *('thob pa, prāpti)*
2 non-acquisition *('thob pa med pa, aprāpti)*
3 similarity of type *(rigs 'thun pa, nikāyasabhāgata)*
4 one having no discrimination *('du shes med pa pa, āsaṃjñika)*
5 absorption without discrimination *('du shes med pa'i snyoms 'jug, asaṃjñisamāpatti)*

6 absorption of cessation *('gog pa'i snyoms 'jug, nirodhasamāpatti)*
7 life faculty *(srog gi dbang po, jīvitendriya)*
8 production *(skye ba, jāti)*
9 aging *(rga ba, jarā)*
10 duration *(gnas pa, sthiti)*
11 impermanence *(mi rtag pa, anityatā)*
12 group of stems *(ming gi tshogs, nāmakāya)*
13 group of words *(tshig gi tshogs, padakāya)*
14 group of letters *(yi ge'i tshogs, vyañjanakāya)*.

16 Bu-dön *(bu ston)* cites Ratnākaraśānti's *Supreme Essence (sārottamā)* as his source for the twelve branches of scripture. They are:

Discourses *(mdo de, sūtra)*
Songs *(dbyangs kyis bsnyad pa, geya)*
Prophecies *(lung du bstan pa, vyākaraṇa)*
Verses *(tshigs su bcad pa, gāthā)*
Purposeful Statements *(ched du brjod pa, udāna)*
Summaries *(gleng gzhi, nidāna)*
Hagiography *(rtogs pa'i brjod pa, avadāna)*
Legends *(de lta bu byung ba, itivṛttaka)*
Birth Stories *(skyes pa rabs, jātaka)*
Vast Texts *(shin tu rgyas pa, vaipulya)*
Miraculous Qualities *(rmad du byung ba'i chos, adbhuta-dharma)*
Delineations *(gtan la phab par bstan pa, upadeśa)*.

For a brief description of the subject matter of each of the branches and an explanation of how they are included into the three scriptural collections *(sde snod, piṭaka)*, see E. Obermiller, trans., *History of Buddhism by Bu-ston*, Part I (Heidelberg: Heft, 1931), pp. 31-34.

17 The two scriptural collections are those of the Lesser Vehicle and the Great Vehicle. The Sanskrit is:

piṭakatrayaṃ dvayaṃ vā saṃgrahataḥ
kāraṇairnavabhiraṣṭam

See S. Bagchi, ed., *Mahāyāna-Sūtrālaṃkāra of Asaṅga*, Buddhist Sanskrit Texts, No. 13, (Darbhanga: Mithila Institute, 1970), p.55.

18 The four thoughts are:

Thinking of sameness *(mnyam pa nyid la dgongs pa, samatābhiprāya)*

Thinking of another meaning *(don gzhan la dgongs pa, arthāntarābhiprāya)*

Thinking of another time *(dus gzhan la dgongs pa, kālāntarābhiprāya)*

Thinking of a person's thought *(gang zag gi bsam pa la dgongs pa, pudgalāntarābhiprāya).*

The four intentions are:

Intending entry [into the teaching] *(gzhug pa la ldem por dgongs pa, avatāranābhisandhi)*

Intending the [three]characters *(mtshan nyid la ldem por dgongs pa, laksanābhisandhi)*

Intending an antidote *(gnyen po la ldem por dgongs pa, pratipaksābhisandhi)*

Intending translation *(sbyor ba la ldem por dgongs pa/ bsgyur ba la ldem por dgongs pa, pariṇāmābhisandhi).*

Source: Jam-ȳang-shay-b̄a's *Great Exposition of Tenets* also known as *Explanation of 'Tenets', Sun of the Land of Samantabhadra Brilliantly Illuminating All of Our Own and Others' Tenets and the Meaning of the Profound* [*Emptiness*], *Ocean of Scripture and Reasoning Fulfilling All Hopes of All Beings (grub mtha'i rnam bshad rang gzhan grub mtha' kun dang zab don mchod tu gsal ba kun bzang zhing gi nyi ma lung rigs rgya mtsho skye dgu'i re ba kun skong),* (Musoorie: Dalama, 1962), nga 9b.7. Jam-ȳang-shay-b̄a gives Maitreya's *Ornament for the Great Vehicle Sūtras (mdo sde rgyan, sūtrālaṃkāra)* as his source.

19 For a list and brief description of the harmonies of enlightenment, see Jeffrey Hopkins, *Meditation on Emptiness,* pp. 205-206.

20 These are the last two lines of the seventh stanza of the *Friendly Letter.* The text is not extant in Sanskrit. There are three recent translations from the Tibetan, each with commentary. They are: Geshe Lobsang Tharchin and Artemus B. Engle, trans., *Nāgārjuna's Letter* (Dharamsala, India: Library of Tibetan Works and Archives,

1979); Lozang Jamspal, et. al., trans., *Nāgārjuna's Letter to King Gautamīputra* (Delhi: Motilal Banarsidass, 1978); and Leslie Kawamura, trans., *Golden Zephyr* (Emeryville, California: Dharma Publishing, 1975).

21 The Sanskrit is:

tadaudārikasaṃgrahāt
daśa karmapathā ukta yathāyogaṃ
śubhāśubhāḥ

See P. Pradhan, ed., *Abhidharmakośabhāṣyam of Vasubandhu*, p. 238.

22 Bracketed material is from Ge-dun-drup *(dge 'dun grub)*, the First Dalai Lama, *Explanation of* [*Vasubhandu's*] *Excellent "Treasury of Knowledge," Illuminating the Path of Liberation (dam pa'i chos mngon pa'i mdzod kyi rnam par bshad pa thar lam gsal byed)*, (Varanasi: wa na mtho slob dge ldan spyi las khang, 1973), 242.4

23 D̄zong-ka-b̄a *(tsong kha pa)* identifies the basis as "a sentient being who serves as a basis for generating an attitude of harmful intent" *(kun nas mnar sems skye ba'i gzhir gyur pa'i sems can)*. See *The Lam rim chen mo of the incomparable Tsong-kha-pa, with the interlineal notes of Ba-so Chos-kyi-rgyal-mtshan, Sde-drug Mkhan-chen Ngag-dbang-rab-brtan, 'Jam-dbyangs-bshad-pa'i-rdo-rje, and Bra-sti Dge-bshes Rin-chen-don-grub*, (New Delhi: Chos-'phel-legs-ldan, 1972), vol. 1, 323.2.

24 The Sanskrit is:

aṣṭadhā prātimokṣākhyaḥ dravyatastu caturvidhaḥ

See P. Pradhan, ed., *Abhidharmakośabhāṣyam of Vasubandhu*, p. 205.

25 For the Tibetan and Sanskrit terms for these classes of vows, see the glossary. For an enumeration and study of the rules of monastic discipline of the Mahāsaṃghika and Mūlasarvāstivādin schools of Indian Buddhism, see Charles S. Prebish, *Buddhist Monastic Discipline*, (University Park, Pennsylvania: Pennsylvania State University Press, 1975).

26 The Sanskrit is:

śamathena vipaśyanāsuyuktaḥ

kurute kleśavināśamityavetya śamathaḥ
prathamamṃgaveṣaṇīyaḥ sa ca loke
nirapekṣayābhiratyā

See Vidhushekara Bhattacharya, ed., *Bodhicaryāvatāra*, Bibliotheca Indica Vol. 280 (Calcutta: the Asiatic Society, 1960), p. 136.

27 The Sanskrit is:

pañcadoṣaprahāṇā 'ṣṭasaṃkārā 'sevanā 'nvayā

See Ramchandra Pandeya, ed., *Madhyānta-Vibhāga-Śāstra*, (Delhi: Motilal Banarsidass, 1971), p. 129.

28 The Sanskrit is:

kausīdyamavavādasya sammoṣo laya uddhavaḥ
asaṃ skāro 'tha saṃkāraḥ pañca doṣā ime matāḥ

See Pandeya, ed., p. 130.

29 The Sanskrit is:

āśrayo 'thāśritastasya nimittaṃ phalameva ca
ālambano 'sammoṣo layauddhatyā 'nubuddhyanā
tadapāyā 'bhisaṃskāraḥ śāntau praśaṭhavāhitā

See Pandeya, ed., pp. 130-131. The bracketed material is drawn from *The Lam rim chen mo of the incomparable Tsong-kha-pa, with the interlineal notes of Ba-so Chos-kyi-rgyal-mtshan, Sde-drug Mkhan-chen Ngag-dbang-rab-brtan, 'Jam-dbyangs-bshad-pa'i-rdo-rje, and Bra-sti Dge-bshes Rin-chen-don-grub,* vol.2, 36.2-.6 and 89.6-90.2.

30 The Sanskrit is:

nibadhyālambane cittaṃ tatpravedhaṃ [vāhaṃ] na vikṣipet
avagamyāśu vikṣepaṃ tasmin pratiharetpunaḥ
pratyātmaṃ saṃkṣipeccittamuparyupari buddhimān
tataścara [da]mayeccitaṃsamādhau guṇadarśanāt
arati śamayettasminvikṣepadoṣadarśanāt
abhidhyādaurmanasyādīnvyutthitān śamayettathā
tataśca sābhisaṃskārāṃ citte svarasavāhitāṃ
labhetānabhisaṃskārān [rāṃ] tadabhyāsātpunaryatiḥ

See S. Bagchi, ed., *Mahāyāna-Sūtrālaṃkāra of Asaṅga*, Buddhist Sanskrit Texts, No. 13, (Darbhanga: Mithila Institute, 1970), p.89.

The numbers in parentheses correspond to the nine mental abidings as identified in *The Lam rin chen mo of the incomparable Tsong-kha-pa, with the interlineal notes of Ba-so Chos-kyi-rgyal-mtshan, Sde-drug Mkhan-chen Ngag-dbang-rab-brtan, 'Jam-dbyangs-bshad-pa'i-rdo-rje, and Bra-sti Dge-bshes Rin-chen-don-grub,* vol.2, 93.4–103.6.

31 For a description of the concentrations and formless absorptions and how they are attained, see the eighth chapter of Vasubandhu's *Treasury of Knowledge* in Louis de la Vallée Poussin, trans., *L'Abhidharmakośa de Vasubandhu,* Tome V, (Bruxelles: Institut Belge des Hautes Études Chinoises, 1971), pp. 127-225. See also Lati Rinbochay, Denma Lochö Rinbochay, Leah Zahler, Jeffrey Hopkins, *Meditative States in Tibetan Buddhism,* (London: Wisdom Publications, 1983), pp. 92-133.

32 For a translation into French, see W. Rahula, *Le Compendium de la Super-Doctrine Philosophie,* (Paris: École Française d'Extrême Orient, 1971), p.112. For the Sanskrit, see P. Pradhan, ed., *Abhidharma Samuccaya,* (Santiniketan: Visva-Bharati, 1950) and N. Tatia, ed., *Abhidharma-samuccayabhāṣyam,* Tibetan-Sanskrit Works Series, No. 17, (Patna: K.B. Jayaswal Research Institute, 1976).

33 See *Meditative States in Tibetan Buddhism,* pp. 102-115.

34 This is also called stabilization *(ting nge 'dzin, samādhi).*

35 The Sanskrit is:

> pañcādye tarkacārau ca prītisaukhyasamādhayaḥ
> prītyādayaḥprasādaśca dvitīye 'ṅgacatuṣṭayam
> tṛtīye pañca tūpeksā smṛ tiḥ prajñā sukhaṃ sthitiḥ
> catvāryante 'sukhāduḥ khopekṣ āsmṛ tisamādhayaḥ

See P. Pradhan, ed., *Abhidharmakośabhāsyam of Vasubandhu* (Patna: Jayaswal Research Insitute, 1975), pp. 437-438.

36 For a full description of the concentrations and the mode of proceeding from one concentration to the next, see *Meditative States in Tibetan Buddhism,* pp. 146-204.

37 See *Madhayamakāvatāra par Candrakīrti,* publiée par Louis de la Vallée Poussin, Bibliotheca Buddhica IX (Osnabrück: Biblio Verlag, 1970), p. 233. Chandrakīrti

quotes this stanza in his *Prasannapadā (Mūlamadhyamakakārikās de Nāgārjuna avec la Prasannapadā Commentaire de Candrakīrti* publiée par Louis de la Vallée Poussin, Bibliotheca Buddhica IV, p.340). The Sanskrit is:

satkāyadṛṣṭiprabha[v]ānaśeṣān kleśāṃśca doṣāṃśca dhiyā vipaśyan
ātmānamasyā viṣayaṃ ca buddhvā yogī karotyātmaniṣedhameva.

38 P5284, Vol. 101 1.1.8.

39 The Sanskrit is:

kalpitaṃ bhāvamaspṛṣṭvā tadabhāvo na gṛhyate

See Vidhushekara Bhattacharya, ed., *Bodhicaryāvatāra,* Bibliotheca Indica Vol. 280 (Calcutta: the Asiatic Society, 1960), p.221.

40 For a description of these reasonings, see Jeffrey Hopkins, *Meditation on Emptiness,* pp. 125-196.

41 The four mindful establishments are the mindfulness of body, feelings, thoughts, and phenomena. The four thorough abandonings are the abandoning of afflictions already produced, the non-production of afflictions not yet produced, the increasing of pure phenomena already produced, and the production of pure phenomena not yet produced. The four legs of emanation are aspiration, effort, thought, and analysis.

42 The five faculties and the five powers are faith, effort, mindfulness, meditative stabilization, and wisdom.

43 The sixteen aspects of the four truths are:

True Sufferings

1 impermanence
2 misery
3 emptiness
4 selflessness

True Origins

5 cause
6 origin
7 strong production
8 condition

True Cessations

9 cessation
10 pacification
11 auspicious highness
12 definite emergence
Truth Paths
13 path
14 suitability
15 achievement
16 deliverance.

For a description, see Jeffrey Hopkins, *Meditation on Emptiness,* pp. 292-296.

44 The Sanskrit is:

paricchedo 'tha samprāptiḥ parasambhāvanā tridhā
vipakṣapratipakṣaśca mārgasyāṅgaṃ tadaṣṭadhā

See Ramchandra Pandeya, ed., *Madhyānta-Vibhāga-Śāstra,* (Delhi: Motilal Banarsidass, 1971), p.136.

45 For a fuller description of the Lesser Vehicle path, see the sixth chapter of Vasubandhu's *Treasury of Knowledge* in Louis de la Vallée Poussin, trans., *L'Abhidharmakośa de Vasubandhu,* Tome IV (Bruxelles: Institut Belge des Hautes Études Chinoises, 1971).

46 For a fuller description of the ten Bodhisattva grounds, see M. Honda, "An Annotated Translation of the 'Daśabhūmika'", *Studies in Southeast and Central Asia,* Śatapitaka Series 74, (New Delhi: 1968), pp. 115-276.

47 For a fuller description of the Bodhisattva path, see E. Obermiller, "The Doctrine of Prajñāpāramitā as Exposed in the Abhisamayālaṃkāra of Maitreya", *Acta Orientalia,* Vol. XI, Parts 1 and 2, (E.J. Brill, 1932), pp. 1-134, 335-354 and Jeffrey Hopkins, *Meditation on Emptiness,* pp. 29-123.

48 P4530, Vol. 81, 115.2.5-115.2.6; Tripiṭakamāla's own commentary on this goes through to 118.2.6.

49 For a discussion of the practice of deity yoga, see Tsong-ka-pa, *Tantra in Tibet,* (London: George Allen and Unwin, 1977).

50 P11, Vol. 1, 234.1.5-234.1.6.

51 For descriptions of the four sets of tantras, see *Tantra in*

Tibet, pp. 151-164, 201-210 and F.D. Lessing and A. Wayman, *Introduction to the Buddhist Tantrica Systems* (Delhi: Motilal Banarsidass, 1978), pp. 101-337. For an exposition of the practice of Action and Performance Tantra, see Tsong-ka-pa, *The Yoga of Tibet,* (London: George Allen and Unwin, 1981).

52 The Highest Yoga Tantra practice of the Great Seal is described in Kelsang Gyatso, *Clear Light of Bliss,* (London: Wisdom Publications, 1982).

53 The Sanskrit is:

svabhāvikaḥsasaṃbhogo nairmāṇikc 'parastathā
dharmakāyaḥ sakāritraścaturdhā samudīritaḥ

See Th. Stcherbatsky and E. Obermiller, ed., *Abhisamayālankāra-Prajñāpāramitā-Upadeśa-Śāstra,* Bibliotheca Buddhica XXIII, (Osnabrück: Biblio Verlag, 1970), p.3.

54 In the life of the Buddha contained in Bu-ḍön's *History of Buddhism,* there appears the story, drawn from the *Brief Scriptures on Discipline ('dul ba phran tshegs kyi gzhi, vinayakṣudravastu)* of how the Buddha, on the evening of his death, subdued the pride of Sunanda, a king of the Gandharvas, skilled in playing the lute. Citing Obermiller's translation (Part II, pp. 59-60):

> In order to subdue [Sunanda], the Lord took a lute with one thousand strings and a frame of Vaidurya stone. Then having transformed himself into a Gandharva, he appeared before the doors of Sunanda and proposed a match in the skill of music. He gradually cut off all the strings with the exception of one, but the sound nevertheless remained the same. Finally, the Buddha cut off the single string that remained, likewise. But in the empty space the sound continued to ring as before. The pride of Sunanda was thus humiliated and he was greatly astonished. The Teacher then appeared in his true form, and Sunanda, full of faith, made his salutations and sat down in order to hear the Teaching. And, as the Lord preached the Doctrine to him, Sunanda came to the intuition of the Truth.

55 Shākyamuni Buddha, after his attainment of Buddhahood in the Heavily Adorned Pure Land and before he entered the womb of Mahamāya on earth, took birth in the Joyous Pure Land as the god Shvetaketu. See Obermiller, Part I, p.136.

56 The thirty-two marks and eighty minor marks are listed in Edward Conze, trans., *Abhisamayālaṃkāra,* Serie Orientale Roma VI (Rome, Is.M.E.O, 1954), pp. 98-102.

57 The sixty-four qualities of melodious speech are listed by Bu-dön in his *History*. See Obermiller, Part I, pp.26-30.

58 For traditional histories of the earlier and later disseminations of the Buddhist doctrine in Tibet, see E. Obermiller, trans., *History of Buddhism by Bu-ston,* Part II (Heidelberg: Heft, 1932), pp. 181-224 and George N. Roerich, trans., *The Blue Annals* (Delhi: Motilal Banarsidass, 1976).

59 The Dalai Lama pointed out that Ḡa-dam-ḇa or "Word As Practical Instruction School" *(bka' gdams pa)* is so called because they understand all of the Conqueror Buddha's word as instructions for practice *(rgyal ba'i bka' thams cad gdams ngag du go ba);* that the Dzok-chen-ḇa or "Great Completeness School" *(rdzogs chen pa)* is so called from the point of view that all faults are primordially purified and all good qualities are primordially completed or perfected *(skyon ye nas dag pa, yon tan ye nas rdzogs pa);* that the Chak-chen-ḇa or "Great Seal School" *(phyag chen pa)* is so called from the viewpoint that all of cyclic existence and nirvana do not pass beyond this [fundamental innate mind of clear light] *('khor 'das thams cad de las 'da 'ba med pa);* and that the Shi-jay-ḇa or "Pacifying School" *(zhi byed pa)* is so called because of having the means for pacifying suffering *(sdug bsngal zhi byed).*

60 For a traditional biography of Padmasambhava, see Yeshe Tsogyal, *The Life and Liberation of Padmasambhava,* 2 vols. (Berkeley: Dharma Publishing, 1978).

61 For a traditional biography of Mar-ḇa, see Tsang Nyon

Heruka, *The Life of Marpa the Translator* (Boulder: Prajna Press, 1982).

62 For a traditional biography of Nāropa, see Herbert V. Guenther, *The Life and Teachings of Nāropa,* (London: Oxford University Press, 1963).

63 For a traditional biography of Mi-la-re-b̄a, see Lobsang P. Lhalungpa, trans., *The Life of Milarepa,* (New York: Dutton Press, 1977).

64 For a study of the life and times of Atīsha, see Alaka Chattopadhyaya, *Atīśa and Tibet* (Delhi: Motilal Banarsidass, 1981).

65 For a traditional biography of D̄zong-ka-b̄a, see Robert Thurman, ed., *The Life and Teachings of Tsong Khapa,* (Dharamsala, India: Library of Tibetan Works and Archives, 1982), pp. 3-39.

66 The three analyses are, roughly speaking, to determine that a passage is not contradicted by direct perception, inference, or other literally acceptable scriptures.

67 The first edition concludes with a publisher's colophon:

> The Great Refuge and Protector [His Holiness the Fourteenth Dalai Lama] composed this *Opening the Eye of New Awareness* for young people of clear minds of the religious land of Tibet and for scholars of East and West who wish to know the stainless teaching of the Supramundane and Victorious Buddha so that they may easily understand the essence of what was first set forth by the Teacher Buddha – the meanings that he realized and perceived through the power of his own knowledge – and of the innumerable scriptures by Indian scholars and adepts commenting on Buddha's thought. The book is intended as a means for easily understanding the presentations of the Buddhist world view and for implementing this in practicing the view, meditation, and behavior. [The Tibetan text was] published by the Office of Religious Affairs of the government of Tibet on the fifteenth day of the third month of the Tibetan year of the Water Tiger 937 (May 8, 1963). May it bring virtue in all directions at all times!

Publisher's Acknowledgement

The publisher thanks Don Courtney, Harald Desjarlais, Richard Gere, the Barry Hershey Foundation, John Hood and Axel and Christine Leblois for sponsoring the printing of this book. Through their merit may all sentient beings reach enlightenment right away!